Don't Get Mad. Write!

Don't Get Mad. Write!

How to Write Effective Letters of Complaint

Bruce West

The publishers acknowledge with thanks the legal assistance of Martin Gleeson in preparing the United Kingdom edition.

First published in Canada in 1992 by Stoddart Publishing Co Ltd, 34 Lesmill Road, Toronto, Canada.

This revised edition first published in Great Britain in 1993 by Kogan Page Ltd, 120 Pentonville Road, London N1 9JN.

British Library Cataloguing in Publication Data

A CIP record for this book is available from the British Library.

ISBN 0-7494-1018-7 PB
ISBN 0-7494-1348-4 HB

Printed and bound in Great Britain by
Clays Ltd, St Ives plc.

Contents

Introduction

Every single day, people from all walks of life suffer numerous injustices at the hands of bank clerks, insurance clerks, mechanics, retailers and others. A silk blouse loses its colour on the very first wash. A new car breaks down just minutes after leaving the showroom. Many innocent victims seethe in silence, or seek the sympathy of friends, neighbours, and relatives. Some may even complain to the offender, by phone or in person, only to encounter frustration. But few use the most effective communication tool of all – the letter.

Don't get mad . . . write!

In this age of sophisticated electronic communications, the art of writing letters has become almost obsolete. The basics of letter writing are no longer emphasized or even taught in our schools. People send memos to one another via electronic mail systems or reach for the telephone. The mighty pen has bene replaced by the push button. But is the push button mightier than the pen? Not in the realm of lodging complaints. When you need to negotiate from a position of strength, when you want to maintain control of a situation, a carefully composed letter will always be immeasurably more effective.

The telephone is, of course, useful for most mundane personal and business purposes, and it does have its advantages: local calls are cheap, contact is usually immediate, and using it has become second nature. But consider the disadvantages: the person you wish to speak to will undoubtedly be 'unavailable', or be so articulate and accomplished at fielding complaints that you will be left tongue-tied; if you do succeed in lodging your point of view, there is no written guarantee that your efforts will be rewarded; and if further action is required you will have no record of the conversation. In my experience, women are particularly ignored, both over the telephone and in person, even (especially?) by other women.

What follows will, I hope, instill in you new confidence and respect for the written word. My humorous book, *Outrageously Yours*, published in Canada by General Publishing in 1986, and in the USA by Putnam Publishing in 1987, illustrates the astonishing results of deliberate and blatant tongue-in-cheek correspondence. This latest tome provides step-by-step instructions you can use to solve virtually any problem, however daunting. I have practised these procedures over many years, and they have almost invariably produced the desired result, often, dare I confess, to my complete astonishment!

The primary intention of this book is to show you how to solve consumer disputes without going to court. Occasionally, however, legal action may be required, and appropriate steps for seeking restitution through the small claims court are included in Chapter 10. If you feel your particular circumstances warrant legal advice, the same chapter includes some pointers for selecting a solicitor.

1

The Basics

Most disputes result from a failure to communicate effectively. Effective communication occurs when concise information is transmitted clearly, and to the right person. Furthermore, that information must be worded so that the recipient will be receptive to it.

The strategy

Satisfactorily solving all that life tends to throw one's way requires calm and careful planning – a strategy like the one outlined below. In the following chapters we will see how this strategy can be adapted to different situations. It is essential to become familiar with the basic steps and to understand the reasons for practising them in relevant order.

1. **Stay calm**. This is essential, although it may not always be easy. Staying calm allows you to plan your approach, to maintain respect, and to stay in control. If you burst into the offending establishment at peak business hours, accuse all the staff of fraud and theft, and then threaten to burn the place down, to sue all concerned, and to set up pickets warning future customers of the conspiracy to defraud them of their life savings, a sympathetic review will not be forthcoming, and you will achieve nothing.
2. **Visualize your opponent's reaction**. Before planning your approach, picture your opponent's reaction to your confrontation. Putting yourself in the other's shoes enables you to plan your approach.
3. **Assess the situation**. Next, you need to determine if there *really is* a problem. The best way to do this is to telephone or visit the offender. In many cases, the dispute can be resolved during this initial meeting. However, if not, and further action is required, it is important to stay calm, make careful mental or written notes of what transpires, and discover the name and status of the person you are dealing with.

Don't make more than one visit or call, because you won't have any record of what was said (although you may be grateful you don't have a record of what you said during a heated argument!). You could be wasting your time speaking to someone who does not have the authority to solve the problem. You might be dealing with a company whose employees are well versed in handling complaints: they keep you on the line while they page someone who has no intention of speaking to you anyway, pass you from colleague to colleague, take messages with the promise that someone will call you back. Waste no more time, for these people are masters of their craft and know that you will soon capitulate through sheer frustration, leaving them the winners.

If you must leave a message, leave a call-back number that will be answered during normal business hours in order to give the institution every opportunity to get in touch with you. Two days is time enough for a call to be returned.

4. **Deal with the most senior person available**. Often, of course, you can resolve a problem with the employee you dealt with originally. However, at the first sign of non-cooperation, you should firmly request to talk to the most senior person with the authority to help you. If that person is not available, you should refuse to deal further with the employee and take your leave.

5. **Request the name of the managing director**. Before you leave, you should request the full name of the MD of the organization as well as his office address. This may, in some circumstances, prompt a reconsideration of your request for a refund, especially if you look determined to make use of the information.

6. **Confirm the information**. When you get home, confirm the name and address of the MD. This is essential. Spelling anyone's name wrong does not create an endearing impression. Besides which, it makes you look amateurish, and no one is impressed by amateurs, least of all company MDs. There is no need to be nervous about verifying this information. All it takes is a simple phone call to the store or head office of the institution.

7. **Write to the MD**. Why the MD? There are numerous reasons:
   - You will have the best chance of success. With the possible exception of the chairman, the MD is the most important person in an organization and has absolute authority over everyone else in the company.
   - You eliminate wasting valuable time writing to someone who is not empowered to deal with your problem.

- You give the MD the opportunity of personal contact with a customer, possibly a refreshing experience!
- The MD may be unaware that the company is selling faulty merchandise or providing shoddy service, which means lost customers (ie, money), and will undoubtedly appreciate your comments, correct the problem from the top, and consequently eliminate future complaints.
- If you eventually need to begin a court case, your case will be much stronger if you have corresponded with top managenemt.
- By expressing your annoyance and inconvenience in writing to the MD, you subtly include 'damages' in your claim. An MD will want to uphold the company's reputation (or if busy with more pressing matters, will simply want to get rid of you), and will probably refund all your money, even if you're not entitled to a full refund.

The letter

Your letter must be carefully phrased to suit the circumstances, and it must summarize concisely the complaint and state clearly what your expectations are – an MD doesn't have the time to read your life story. Furthermore, the MD will be more receptive if your tone reflects someone of equal status, someone who expects immediate action. Another advantage of writing is that, no matter what your education or background, you can communicate with anyone in the world on equal terms.

Once you get into the habit of writing instead of getting mad, you will write with greater fluidity and confidence. After a while, you will regard MDs as no more than ordinary employees with an obligation to give you the service you deserve – which is, of course, a perfectly realistic expectation.

Never correspond by hand. *Always type any correspondence.* Even if your handwriting is excellent, it makes your letter look amateur. Business correspondence is always typed, and you are communicating with a business person. If you do not own a typewriter or word processor, borrow one, persuade a friend to help you, or hire a professional typing or word-processing service listed in the telephone directory. (Don't forget to include this expense when you send your claim to the company.)

Your letter should be typed on good quality A4 paper. There is no need to use letterhead, unless you have it, but your paper and envelope should look businesslike: white or a soft neutral shade best convey the message that you mean business.

Before posting any correspondence, make a photocopy and keep it in a file along with any future correspondence as well as the bill or invoice for the goods or service, expense receipts, and any pertinent notes.

When you send your letter, make sure you address your envelope properly.

Low-Graad Manufacturing Ltd
232 Industrial Park Road
Dowtfulle
HS2 2VP

For the attention of Aryu Cheep, Managing Director

PRIVATE AND CONFIDENTIAL

If the name of the addressee is placed apart from the company name, it will stand out. Putting PRIVATE AND CONFIDENTIAL on the envelope will ensure that it is opened and read by the addressee (or by the personal secretary, who will forward it in any event).

There are several ways to send your letter: by ordinary mail, special delivery, recorded delivery, courier, or fax. Fax or mail is cheapest, and the letter will normally reach its destination. Faxed letters have an air of urgency ablout them that could mean more immediate action. The fax machine will record the time and date of the transmission and the fax number of the recipient. But a fax may be received by a clerk who sends it to the customer service department instead of the MD, or it could be left in a pile by the machine for days, so you should always send your letter by mail, too. If you are concerned about the reliability of the postal service in your area, you could send the letter by special delivery or recorded delivery, or use a courier. I post my letters and have not encountered any problems. (When I do, you can be sure I won't get mad – I'll write to the head of the Post Office!)

The expenses

Ask for receipts for all your expenses – postage, stationery, telephone calls, typing or courier services, transport costs – and keep careful records of the amount of time you spend dealing with any problem. You will invoice the offending institution for your time and expenses as part of your claim.

How much should you charge for your time? When you calculate your hourly rate, I suggest you use an hourly rate of four times your normal pay – more if your job is not well paid! You need not specify your rate on the invoice – just the total. I charge £30 an hour when I invoice 'customers', and to date this has never been questioned (I type with two fingers, so my invoices are scarely a bargain!). One of the most persuasive methods of ensuring that institutions treat their customers well is to relieve them of some money every time they fail to do so.

Taking your complaint further

If you have exhausted all your possibilities of complaining to the offending institution, when you have written to the chairman and received a negative response each time (or no response at all!), then there are usually other ways of taking your complaint further.

Thanks to the efforts of enlightened legislators and in particular to the Office of Fair Trading, most trades and professions have grouped themselves together into associations, have adopted codes of practice, have required their members to adhere to those codes and have provided for ways of resolving disputes between the trader and the customer. So you should find out whether the person, shop or company you are in dispute with is a member of one (or maybe more) trade associations. Look on their shop windows, their letters, their invoices, their receipts or simply ask them. Find out the address of the association (the Office of Fair Trading will be able to give you this if you cannot discover it), find out if there is a code of practice and get a copy of it. Look carefully at it to see if you think the trader has breached the code in his dealings with you. If he has, this will give you extra ammunition to throw at him.

See if there is a complaints procedure and/or an arbitration procedure and think about using this as an alternative to court. Will you be bound by the arbitrator's decision? Normally not, and you can then still go to court afterwards if you are not satisfied with the outcome of the arbitration. Let the trader know that you are aware of the trade association and its code of practice. This in itself will sometimes make him capitulate when he realizes he is dealing with someone with more tenacity than usual.

A list of some of the many trade and professional associations is given in the 'Useful Addresses' section on page 172. The Office of Fair Trading, your local Trading Standards Department, your local Citizens' Advice Bureau, consumer advice agency or other advice agency ought to be able to help you find names and addresses.

A second avenue for taking your complaints further is to use consumer programmes on television and magazines. If you believe you have been particularly badly dealt with, you may consider writing to a television programme like BBC1's *Watchdog*, and the mere threat of this to a well-known public institution with a reputation to protect will often produce immediate cooperation. The Consumers' Association is another avenue. Even if you are not a member, you can always threaten the shop with writing to them.

Magazines of the more practical kind which specialize in the particular area of life about which you are in dispute will sometimes be interested to hear of any problems that you may be having. Again, tell the trader that you are going to write to them, as the mere threat will sometimes work.

2

It's Your Money: Taking on the Banks

How often have you or someone you know been the victim of an error committed by a bank? An error can result in all kinds of headaches: a returned cheque, an unexpected service charge, or a missed standing order.

Banks routinely employ staff who are completely inexperienced in even the most rudimentary clerical procedures, because banks save on wages by employing unskilled help or because there is a shortage of skilled labour. Whatever the reason, it saves the banks a great deal of money at the expense and inconvenience of the customer, who is increasingly treated as a source of great irritation rather than the essential and respected reason for the banks' existence!

When an error is discovered, you can spend days trying to find someone in the branch with the intelligence to understand the nature of the error, and yet more time locating someone else who is capable of correcting it. At the end of it all, you consider yourself fortunate to have achieved a belated reversal of the mistake, a mistake that may have cost you dearly in time and reputation.

Despite the power they appear to hold over the mere mortal customer, banks are entirely responsible for their mistakes, just like any other organization or individual, and it is relatively easy to extract compensation from them. At least, it is reassuring to know that they can afford to pay for their mistakes!

Incorrect debit

Let's assume you are the owner of a house, with the inevitable mortgage to constantly remind you of your most expensive asset. The mortgagee relieves your bank account of the repayment by standing order.

Each month you deposit your pay cheque and, having calculated the amount that will be debited for the mortgage you then plan your budget for the balance.

Last month, you received a notice from the mortgagee advising you of a minor adjustment – it seems they underestimated the amount required when the mortgage was renewed a year ago. The additional charge is very small, £8, and you have adjusted your budget accordingly. You write to the bank, telling them to amend the standing order.

Unfortunately, the bank has made an error, and your account is, in fact, being relieved of *£80* a month. You, however, are blissfully spending the money, which will no longer be available to cover your cheques.

The first indication that anything is amiss arrives in your letter box some 12 days after the mortgage payment due date. To your amazement it is a letter from the holder of your mortgage, informing you that the monthly standing order payment was not paid by your bank and that a new debit will be made, together with an additional administrative charge of £10. Naturally, you are upset.

Now, you begin to correct matters in the most expedient manner, making careful notes of all that transpires. First of all, check the letter that you sent the bank to ensure that the mistake is definitely the bank's, and that you did not incorrectly state the adjustment. Verify, too, that you haven't written any cheques that you have not recorded in your cheque book stubs.

Once you establish that the error is unquestionably not yours, it is time to phone the bank. Ask for whoever is responsible for standing orders administration. Explain the circumstances carefully, and request a written explanation of why the error occurred as well as an account of what will be done to rectify the matter and compensate you for your inconvenience.

If you don't get through, and your call isn't returned after two days, it is time to write to the manager. (You have, of course, confirmed the spelling of his name.) You write as follows:

---

24 Dettor Lane
Uptite
Inutopia
FG3 2BW

Mr Watt A Cashgrasper
Manager
The Luting Bank
1 Usurer Place
Amor
Gagee
SC9 3LT

22 February 1993

Dear Mr Cashgrasper

On 15 January, I received a letter from my mortgage company referring to my mortgage, number 345234, informing me that the standing order for £478.87 had not been paid. I telephoned your branch to find out why it had not been paid. I was told that I did not have enough money to cover the additional £80 increase in the debit amount. I pointed out that this was hardly surprising since the amount in question was some £72 in excess of the sum notified (see enclosed copy) and allowed for in my account balance.

The clerk concerned was unable to offer an explanation, but said she would 'check with her supervisor' and call back in a few minutes. To date, I have received no further communication.

Kindly forward an immediate and full explanation.

Any charges and expenses I incur as a consequence of your negligence will be invoiced to your bank for full payment.

Yours sincerely

Broak Kliyent

Encl

Your letter may not receive an immediate reply for numerous reasons: the manager may be away on business; he may have passed the case to a subordinate; there may be postal delays, and so on.

However, you are not accustomed to being kept in the dark by mere branch managers! If you have not received a reply in, say, ten days, it is time to send a reminder to show that you mean business. Your reminder will be worded thus:

---

5 March 1993

Dear Mr Cashgrasper

May I expect your reply to my letter regarding the standing order for my mortgage, number 345234, of 22 February, in the not too distant future?

Yours sincerely

Broak Kliyent

If you still haven't received a reply in a further ten days, then a letter to the chairman at the Head Office is in order. Such a step would, I hope, not be necessary, since the preceding letters are all that are normally required to produce results. The chairman will naturally be pleased to hear how his bank is performing in these competitive times!

---

24 Dettor Lane
Uptite
Inutopia
FG3 2BW

Mr Olden Welthey
Chairman
The Luting Bank
1 Money Street
Richtown
RC6 1TR

15 March 1993

Dear Mr Welthey

On 22 February and again on 5 March, I was obliged to write to your branch manager, Mr Watt A Cashgrasper, at your Gagee branch, concerning the appalling and unpredictable service I am experiencing at the hands of his staff.

Thus far, Mr Cashgrasper has not seen fit to reply to either of my letters. Perhaps you would be good enough to confirm that Mr Cashgrasper has not left your employ and whether his duties include dealing with his correspondence.

I look forward to your earliest reply.

Yours sincerely

Broak Kliyent

You have now sent more than enough correspondence to precipitate a thorough investigation by the highest authority, which should result in a letter of apology, and an admission of liability. If any further correspondence is called for, write to the chairman, even if you have been answered by a branch manager, director, or other executive. Always mention the date and writer of previous correspondence, for example: 'I have received a letter dated 25 March from your Mr Avery Odclerk . . .' Persist until the matter is settled to your satisfaction.

When all has been finalized, add up your expenses and prepare an invoice (don't forget to include your expenses for compiling and sending the invoice). The invoice should be sent to the branch manager.

Broak Kliyent
24 Dettor Lane
Uptite
Inutopia
FG3 2BW

Mr Watt A Cashgrasper
Manager
The Luting Bank
1 Usurer Place
Amor
Gagee
SC9 3LT

2 April 1993

INVOICE

For expenses caused by mismanagement of Account No 345234, resulting in administrative charges, telephone calls, written correspondence, and associated costs.

Total £73.50

Terms: Payment within 14 days. Overdue accounts attract interest at 2% per month.

Within days, you should receive a cheque for £73.50. The bank clearly caused you financial and personal inconvenience, and your firm refusal to accommodate their negligence left them with no option but to pay up. Should they not settle, you would then send a statement, showing interest for the first month. However, as a rule, banks are usually quick at settling accounts, and it is unlikely you will need to send any reminders.

Broak Kliyent
24 Dettor Lane
Uptite
Inutopia
FG3 2BW

The Luting Bank
1 Usurer Place
Amor
Gagee
SC9 3LT

3 May 1993

STATEMENT

Re: Account No 345234

Outstanding balance dated 2 April 1993	£73.50
Interest to 3 May at 2% per month	£1.47
Balance due	£74.97

A second statement, if needed, should be sent with interest compounded for the second month, giving the bank ten days to settle, failing which a complaint to the Banking Ombudsman can be made or you can commence legal action. Issuing a small claims summons is not difficult and is described in detail in Chapter 10.

Failure to notify of cheque returned unpaid

Let us assume you sell your old stereo system through the classified ads for £500.00. The buyer gives you a cheque, produces documentation verifying his address and financial standing, and leaves with the goods. Pleased with your transaction, you deposit the cheque in your account and rush off to purchase the latest in audio equipment.

All is well until, four weeks later, a letter from your bank arrives informing you that the £500.00 cheque for your old stero has been returned unpaid. Horrified, you phone the purchaser only to discover that the number is no longer in service. A quick visit confirms that the crafty purchaser has moved without leaving a forwarding address. You are, of course, upset and vow that next time you will only accept cash or a banker's draft. However, reproaching yourself is not going to recoup the loss. If there is no hope of locating the purchaser, a more promising avenue must be pursued.

Although, obviously, the purchaser is the cause of your dilemma, you may be able to seek damages from the bank. If there was no postal strike or other dispute impeding the performance of your bank, then the four weeks it took for the bank to inform you that the cheque had not been honoured was unreasonable. But before you get carried away with glee, examine the date on the envelope containing the bank's letter. If the postmark is dated three weeks prior to your receiving it, the delay occurred in the post and you will have no claim against the bank.

If the date is recent, however, you may have a case (remember to keep the envelope on file for proof). The amount of time banks take to clear cheques depends on how sophisticated they are, on the location of the bank on which the cheque was issued, and on whether there were intervening weekends or holidays. But four weeks is quite unacceptable. As part of your assessment, you should verify how long it takes your bank to clear a cheque and send an unpaid notice under normal circumstances. In my experience, it takes about seven days.

You examine the letter and its envelope, and see that there is a difference of ten days between their dates. This is all the evidence you need to stake your claim; the bank is clearly at fault.

You can, if you wish, make a telephone call to your branch to register your indignation, but frankly, I think this would be a wasted call. For the 'reward' of not having to admit fault and not having to credit your account with (their) £500.00, they may be prepared to argue extensively, and you will achieve nothing. Far better is to be so outraged by this appalling lack of concern for customers' affairs, that you have no option but to contact the man at the top, and send a copy to the manager of the branch concerned.

---

65 Fairloan Avenue
Upper County
FR2 7SR

Mr Franc Sterling, Managing Director
The Bank of Magna Lucre
Lucre Towers
Goldstreets
LG5 7TP

5 February 1993

Dear Mr Sterling

On 2 January 1993, I deposited into my Account No 5433242, Main Branch, Bank of Magna Lucre, Upper County, a cheque for £500.00. This cheque represented the proceeds for a used stereo system sold earlier that day to a private purchaser. On 30 January, 28 days after the cheque was deposited, I received a letter from my branch informing me that the cheque had been returned unpaid.

I am unable to contact the drawer of the cheque since he moved on 22 January, leaving no forwarding address. Had your bank performed with the efficiency expected of an organization of your stature, as continually claimed in your comprehensive advertising, and not waited four weeks to inform me of this unpaid cheque, I would have been able to collect the £500.00 from my customer. Such gross negligence is quite unacceptable. Kindly, therefore, ensure that my account is credited with the £500.00 in question, without delay.

For your information, the letter, dated 18 January, arrived in an envelope postmarked 28 January. Perhaps this meets your expectation of reasonable performance?

I look forward to your immediate reply.

Yours sincerely

Carole M Uzik
cc Manager, Main Branch, Upper County

You may be surprised to observe that the carbon copy to your branch fails to identify the name of the manager. This is because we are dealing with the managing director at head office, and the status of a mere branch manager is so insignificant that his or her identity is quite unnecessary. As far as we are concerned, whether the letter reaches the

manager or not is unimportant since we would not reply to any communication from that person – our response would be addressed to the MD, 'in reply to the letter dated ——— from your branch manager'. Similarly, should you receive a phone call from the manager, the call should be acknowledged to the MD, although, of course, phone calls should be avoided unless the manager is offering immediate and full capitulation. Firmly request that the caller put any message in writing.

If you have not received a reply within ten days, a sharp reminder to the chairman is in order.

Mr Hugh Jassets, Chairman
The Bank of Magna Lucre
Lucre Towers
Goldstreets
LG5 7TP

15 February 1993

Dear Mr Jassets

On 5 February, I wrote to your managing director, Mr Franc Sterling, concerning the serious mismanagement of my account by your bank. To date, my concerns have yet to be addressed, or even acknowledged.

If Mr Sterling is no longer in your employ, I should be most grateful if you could direct his successor to respond without further delay.

Yours sincerely

Carole M Uzik

Making sure that the chairman is keeping track of his MD is always good insurance. Determined persistence on your part should result in a full credit to your account.

Complaining about banks and building societies

All the high street banks and many others now subscribe to a Code of Practice, which they should adhere to, though their record so far is patchy. Any branch will be able to give you a copy of the Code. If your complaint specifically breaches a term of the Code, you will have good evidence for your complaint.

Most banks and building societies have a complaints procedure, which you can use if you wish. You can set the ball rolling by writing to the branch manager of the bank or building society branch which made the error about which you are complaining. From there follow the complaints procedure.

When you have exhausted the complaints procedure (usually after having written to the head office) then you can ask the Banking Ombudsman or the Building Societies Ombundsman to look at your case. They will make a decision which will be binding on the bank or the building society but not on you. So you can reject the decision if you do not like it. Their services are free of charge.

If you are still dissatisfied, you can take the matter to court. Of course, you need not go through all the procedures mentioned above: you can go straight to court immediately if you wish.

Credit card posted to wrong address

When you move, you are obliged to compile long and tedious lists of friends, utilities, creditors, relatives, and so forth, who need to be informed of your new address. It is essential to notify in good time all the issuers of your credit cards of your new address, for delayed payments can have dire consequences for the card user.

Some card issuers are notorious for failing to take note of change-of-address information. Department stores seem to be particularly lax in this area, so if you think a statement is overdue, call the card issuer concerned to confirm that they are aware of your new whereabouts.

You are not responsible for any transactions covered by your credit card before you have received it. Therefore, if it was stolen or went missing before you received it and is used, you will not have to pay for any of these transactions.

This is not the case with a charge card. You will have a charge card if you are obliged to pay off the full amount of indebtedness each month. With a credit card you need not do this. A charge card will be covered by its own agreement which may or may not make you liable for its loss. Even if you are liable for its loss, it is always worth arguing with the card issuer. The strategy outlined below can be used in both cases.

Your last move is almost forgotten – you have been living in your new home for eight months now. Life is running smoothly, and all your statements are arriving in their usual unwelcome but inevitable fashion. Approximately a month after your move, your card expired; you cut it up and threw it in the bin. The company didn't bother to send you a new card, but you assumed this was because you rarely used it.

To your horror and disbelief, a letter arrives one morning from a collection agency. The tersely worded contents inform you that unless you settle the £729.55 including interest and collection fees owed, legal proceedings will commence within ten days. You phone the person who signed the letter. A stern voice tells you that the account is for purchases over the past six months, and that since you failed to pay any of the statements sent, the credit card company sent the file to the collection agency, who in turn just discovered your new address.

Bewildered, you tell your contact that you do not even own a credit card issued by them. Predictably, the collection agent is unimpressed by your protestations. It is his job to collect the money owed, and your excuses are hardly original – he has heard innumerable variations on your theme throughout his career.

In as calm a voice as you can muster, you ask for a copy of the account to be sent to you at once, and a couple of days later the statement arrives confirming the description of the account given by the agent over the phone.

It is clear that a renewal credit card was sent to your old address and was gratefully intercepted by a keen student of personal frugality! This will have to be confirmed beyond doubt, and used to ensure that you are not held liable for the debt. Your reputation must be rescued unscathed.

Any further attempt to negotiate with the collection agency is unlikely to be productive. You must, therefore, deal directly with the credit card company. However, it would certainly do no harm to send a letter to the MD of the agency, denying any liability whatsoever and informing him that you will be dealing with the credit card company directly from here on. Your letter might look something like this:

---

43 Eagle Drive
Uptown
GH5 3PW

Mrs R U Scrouge, Managing Director
Credigrab Agencies Ltd
Skweaz Towers
Downtown
RT7 4DP

10 February 1993

Dear Mrs Scrouge

Your File No 784352, which claims that I am indebted to Credit Unlimited plc for the amount of £643.78, plus interest and collection, for a total of £729.55, is entirely erroneous and without foundation.

I shall be ensuring that this alleged account is cancelled immediately, through the offices of Mr Costas Lotzferoil, MD of Credit Unlimited plc. You will be advised of the outcome of this issue as soon as it is settled to my satisfaction. Meanwhile, I strongly advise that you refrain from further proceedings.

Yours sincerely

Weil Phixthis

cc Costas Lotzferoil, MD, Credit Unlimited plc

This may stay proceedings for a few days. Should the agency ignore your suggestion, and their persistence has a detrimental effect on your credit standing or causes you financial loss, then you will, of course, claim damages when the dispute is settled.

Meanwhile, you also write to the credit card company.

Mr Costas Lotzferoil, MD
Credit Unlimited plc
High Towers
Crudetown
YH6 2DP

10 February 1993

Dear Mr Lotzferoil

I have received a demand from Credigrab Agencies Ltd, which claims that I am indebted to your company for the amount of £643.78, plus interest, and a collection fee due to the agency, for a total £729.55. Their reference no 784352.

Since I have no business dealings with your company, I am requesting comprehensive written evidence of the premise upon which you base this totally unfounded allegation.

Please be aware that subject to the outcome of this matter, your company and its agents will be held entirely responsible for all expenses I incur as a result of your actions, including damages for my compromised credit rating.

Kindly reply by return of post.
Yours sincerely

Weil Phixthis

cc Mrs R U Scrouge, MD, Credigrab Agencies Ltd

Since you are obliged to deal with two different companies, it is a good idea to send copies of your correspondence to both parties. So far, you don't know how far you may have to go in order to obtain a just conclusion. If it becomes necessary to claim costs, you may have to issue a court summons against one or both parties, in which case your position will be stronger if you can demonstrate to the judge that you made every effort to keep all parties aware of your innocence from the outset.

Within a few days, you receive details of the claim, a brief explanation from the accounts department along with photocopies of 27 receipts for goods, all charged to your account! Close inspection reveals that the card was issued shortly after you moved to your new address, and that the signatures on the receipts bear no resemblance to yours. Included as well are copies of letters from the credit card company, sent to your vacated address, demanding payment of the outstanding amount and finally informing you that the account is being handed over to a collection agency.

You now have all the information you need to see how the claim occurred, and can take appropriate steps to make sure it is quashed, without financial loss or damage to your credit standing. This requires another letter to the credit card company.

Mr Costas Lotzferoil, MD
Credit Unlimited plc
High Towers
Crudetown
YH6 2DP

16 February 1993

Dear Mr Lotzferoil

I am in receipt of a letter dated 12 February, together with enclosures, from your Mr Joe King, in reply to my letter of 10 February.

On 14 June 1992, I informed your organization, in writing, that as of 31 July 1992, I would no longer be residing at 32 Tesco Street, Midtown ER3 2GB, and that all future correspondence should be directed to my new address, as above.

Not only did you choose to ignore my notification, but you apparently sent a new, unsolicited credit card to my vacated address. Not surprisingly, the new card was gratefully received and used by a person unknown over a period of several months.

Since the signatures on the receipts are nothing like my own signature, and your requests for payment were not acknowledged or met, perhaps you could inform me why the receipts were not compared with my authorized signature, which I assume you still have on record. Had you taken this obvious step, and informed the police of the fraudulent use of the card, you might well have apprehended the culprit and saved us both a great deal of time and expense.

Your action has caused me considerable distress and inconvenience. I require an immediate apology, along with confirmation that I am not responsible for this account. I expect Credigrab Agencies Ltd to cease pursuing me, and any credit reference agency to which this account may have been sent to be informed of your error.

As soon as I receive your confirmation that all the above instructions have been complied with, I shall check with all appropriate credit reference agencies. You will be invoiced for my time and expenses in dealing with this matter.

Should I apply for a loan or other credit facility and be refused because my credit rating was adversely affected as a result of your negligence, be aware that I shall expect your organization to furnish me with the loan at the same rate and terms as the declining institution.

I anticipate your immediate reply.

Yours sincerely

Weil Phixthis

cc Mrs R U Scrouge, MD, Credigrab Agencies Ltd (Ref: 784352)

This is a strongly worded letter. Not only is it distressing to be hounded by a collection agency, but a credit rating is important, and it takes very little to destroy years of scrupulous performance. Credit reference agencies have neither the desire nor the ability to investigate the individuals on their registers. Any seemingly bona fide information sent to them is filed against the relevant individual, with no check for accuracy.

You must assume that either the credit card company or Credigrab has already filed your case with the credit reference agency and that you will have to check that the error has been corrected. You can write to an agency at any time asking to see their file on you. A small fee will be charged. The agency must respond within seven days. You can then tell the agency if any of their information is wrong and if you have supporting evidence from the credit card company admitting their mistake then the agency will normally be happy to correct their file. If they will not correct their file you can send a notice of not more than 200 words which states your views on the matter. The agency must put this notice on their file. If they don't you can refer the matter to the Office of Fair Trading for their decision. There are time limits for each step of these procedures, so do not dilly-dally when deciding what to do. The Office of Fair Trading produce a detailed booklet outlining these procedures, which they will supply on request.

Remember to invoice for your expenses.

Weil Phixthis
43 Eagle Drive
Uptown
GH5 3PW

Credit Unlimited plc
High Towers
Crudetown
YH6 2DP

28 February 1993

For the attention of Costas Lotzferoil, MD

INVOICE

For expenses incurred in contesting your erroneous claim for damages resulting from the fraudulent use of an unsolicited credit card by an unknown third party. Your reference no 236 784. Credigrab reference no 784352. Expenses include telephone calls, correspondence, postage, correspondence with credit reference agencies to confirm status, etc.

Total £253.87

Terms: Net 30 days. Overdue accounts attract interest at 1.5% per month.

3

Up in Smoke: Your Car

From the moment you decide to 'invest' in a car, you can be the victim of a host of service professionals, including salesmen and mechanics.

Petrol overcharge on credit card

Since most petrol stations use computerized machinery, there is virtually no margin for error, mechanical or human, in arriving at the correct price for the amount of petrol a customer takes. Yet the service station is probably where you are most vulnerable to a price error. Not that petrol companies, or their employees, intentionally or routinely overcharge their customers, but you can easily pay for petrol consumed by another vehicle.

Say you pull into your favourite service station for a fill-up. The petrol station is busy and you are in a hurry, so you hand over your credit card to the cashier, hurriedly sign the receipt, and leave. When you arrive home in the evening, you turf out your pockets and spot the petrol receipt. You are shocked to discover that you have paid £43.80 for 73 litres of petrol – you clearly recollect stopping the pump at £15.00 or 25 litres. Besides, your car has a maximum tank capacity of only 30 litres!

You are naturally annoyed with yourself; you should have checked the receipt before signing it, as will be made quite clear to you if you go back to complain tomorrow. So is there any point in making a complaint? Well, probably not to the station itself. The cashier, who won't remember you anyway, will be completely powerless to rectify the matter. The owner or manager may not be able to help you either – it may be difficult to trace the error. But you definitely have a case, since it was not you who initiated the error but the employee who served you. You are only responsible for failing to spot the error.

A letter to the MD of the petrol company should prove fruitful. You feel it is a matter of principle. Because you can't prove your claim conclusively, it should be an appeal, rather than a demand.

78 Winding Avenue
Downsvale
HJ4 6WP

Mr Rich Onah, Managing Director
Masev Oil plc
Masev Towers
Octane
BS3 8TQ

19 February 1993

Dear Mr Onah

On the morning of Sunday, 16 February, I filled the petrol tank of my 1988 Rereenda Lorcar, registration number 254 RYH, with 25 litres of 4 star petrol at 60 pence per litre, totalling £15.00. This transaction occurred at your station situated on the corner of Bathover Street and Eastway Street, in Downsvale.

The station was extremely busy at the time and, since I was trying to pay and leave as quickly as possible, in order not to delay the people waiting behind me, I did not examine my credit card receipt when it was presented for signature. To my astonishment and dismay, when I got home that evening and looked at my receipt (photocopy enclosed), I realized that I had paid for fuel amounting to £43.80 for 73 litres. As you can see, the registration number written on the receipt by the cashier matches that of my Lorcar, the tank of which has a maximum capacity of 30 litres.

I do not know whether the mistake was the result of a computer error, or whether I was mistakenly given another customer's bill. I have always received excellent service at this and all your other outlets, and I am sure the error was quite unintentional.

Under the circumstances, I would be most grateful if you could arrange to have the overcharge of £28.80 reimbursed, at your earliest convenience.

Assuring you of my continuing patronage, I thank you in anticipation.

Yours sincerely

Frank Lee Grovling

Encl

Since the amount claimed is very small, and you have given the impression that you are a considerable, reasonable, and above all, regular customer, there is every reason to suppose that a refund will be forthcoming. If not, however, your grounds for any legal redress are doubtful; although the mistake was not yours, you certainly had every opportunity to spot it. There is probably not much point in pursuing the matter further if a refund is not offered, but a letter like this is usually effectivc.

Unauthorized garage repair

There is little doubt that overcharging and needless part replacement does occur in the car repair business. Few people know enough about their vehicle to disagree with an experienced mechanic. Even those who are knowledgeable about car maintenance are at risk because modern technology is producing a new breed of vehicles with computerized circuitry, automatic and electrically operated units, turbochargers, and so on. Even trained mechanics are baffled by the sophisticated equipment they must use to diagnose ailing vehicles. The poor owner has little hope of disputing any estimate.

It helps to learn the correct terminology – one of the best methods of defence is attack. It is unlikely you will be taken advantage of if you tell the mechanic you think the exhaust valves are not seating properly, and ask for the alternative prices for the two viable remedies – fitting a new exchange cylinder head, or grinding and possibly fitting new vales. This will gain you more respect than saying that the engine has been losing power and becoming more difficult to start over several months. Such a vague description might well trigger the installation of a complete exchange engine, at considerably greater expense than any cylinder head work.

Do some research before selecting a garage. The large chains, who consistently advertise specials and who guarantee absolute satisfaction, with warranties that apparently take you well into the next century, are rarely as competent and magnanimous as their reassuring commercials claim. The special offer is invariably a loss leader, meant to lure you on to their jack! The special price will be inflated by the cost of parts that 'need' to be replaced in order to complete the job. If you insist that you just want the advertised job, you will not be given a guarantee for the work done. And, of course, you will be assured that without the complete repair job, your vehicle will be a mobile death trap. As a further incentive, should you decide to take your business elsewhere, you will not be allowed to leave with your vehicle until you pay the inspection charge!

Another alternative, the repair shop of a dealership that specializes in your car make, has the advantage that the mechanics should be familiar with the intricacies of your model. However, there are disadvantages here, too. Dealerships have inflexible pricing policies – if the book rate for a repair is two hours, that is what you will pay, even if the job only takes 45 minutes. They tend to replace complete units instead of a faulty part in the same unit, and they are more likely to replace a part than repair it. They use only genuine replacement parts made by (or for) the manufacturer of your vehicle, which may be sound policy, but can be expensive. The dealership will tell you that more economical 'clone' parts are inferior.

Worth investigating are independent garages. They rely on word of mouth from satisfied customers, so the quality of their service is usually excellent. Their labour rates may be flexible and, since they don't have to buy their parts from one source, they are probably able to supply cheaper parts. A local resident who uses a particular garage should be able to advise you about their reliability and integrity.

Whichever you choose, it's worth doing a little investigation. An ounce of prevention is worth a ton of cure in the car repair business.

Assume you are on your way to an important meeting when your car develops an acute problem, and you just make it to a nearby garage. The owner of the garage tells you that it sounds like the carburettor is suffering from fuel starvation, and that if you sign the work authorization, he will check it out later in the morning and call you with the diagnosis and estimate. You have no alternative, so you leave your car, catch a cab, and head off to your meeting, hoping that whatever is wrong can be repaired quickly and inexpensively.

Despite the inauspicious start to the morning, your meeting is short and you arrive at your office just before eleven. There is no message for you from the garage, so you immediately call them. The owner tells you that the fuel pump is badly corroded and only works intermittently. The price for a new pump, including labour, will be approximately £280.00. He promises to have it ready for you six o'clock. You give him the go-ahead.

Just before six, you arrive at the garage, full of anticipation at the prospect of being reunited with your faithful conveyance, brought back to unaccustomed youthful performance for the not unreasonable sum of £280.00. Your initial joy disappears when you are presented with a bill for £734.65, which is somewhat in excess of the amount agreed to over the telephone!

In deep shock, you examine the bill and discover that the price for fitting the fuel pump has mysteriously increased to £295.00. Furthermore, your car has been fitted with an exchange carburettor, for an additional surprise of £439.65! Immediately, you question the garage owner about the increase in price for the pump, and the reason for changing the carburettor without prior notification and agreement. He offers a reasonable explanation for the additional cost of the pump. The carburettor, however, is a different matter. You were given a definite and binding estimate for installing a pump, with no indication that anything further would be required. The garage owner explains that even with the new pump, the car's performance did not improve. The mechanic made some adjustments to the carburettor, but it, too, was in such bad shape that it needed replacing.

You argue, quite rightly, that since the garage did not have your authority to do the additional work, you are not responsible for paying for it. By now, the owner is less than sympathetic to your reaction. He tells you that unless the bill is paid in full, the car will not be permitted to leave the premises.

In any dispute over a bill, it is to your advantage to pay the amount claimed, to prove both that you are acting in good faith and that you are solvent. You can indicate that you do not agree to your liability by writing 'paid under protest' on the invoice, cheque, or credit card receipt.

You reluctantly agree to pay. But how should you pay? You should not write a cheque and then call your bank first thing in the morning to put a stop payment on it. It is a criminal offence to pay by cheque with the intention of stopping it, and although it is unlikely that you would be charged or convicted, nevertheless, it would not enhance your credibility should you have to go to court. The garage could argue that the reason you disputed the amount was that you didn't have sufficient funds to cover the necessary work, and a stopped cheque would tend to confirm these suspicions. Also, if you were to stop payment on the cheque, the garage would probably initiate proceedings against you, which would damage your credit rating and create a negative impression on a judge.

Meanwhile back at the garage, you have decided to pay by credit card. You have little choice, since the garage predictably enough has refused your cheque. You write 'paid under protest' on the receipt, then you depart in your refurbished conveyance. Later that evening, with your car safely parked at home, you plan your campaign to recover the amount overcharged.

According to the huge sign in the forecourt, the garage sells petrol produced by Supafume Petroleum. However, the invoice reveals that the garage bears the name A V Ridge Wrench Auto. Supafume may not be legally liable for the actions of A V Ridge Wrench Auto, but they will be concerned about damages to their hard-earned reputation and may put pressure on the garage owner to refund your money or make good itself. You will more likely receive a concerned and responsible reaction from a large company than from an independent garage, even if it is not directly responsible for the actions of the garage. The petrol company stands to make a great deal of money from you during your motoring life expectancy – they won't want to lose you as a customer. Therefore, you write to the MD of Supafume Petroleum.

---

76 Drive Avenue
Lower Ridges
KW4 7ZR

Mr Hy Pumprise, MD
Supafume Petroleum Ltd
1 Octane Boulevard
Welltown
TH3 3QR

20 February 1993

Dear Mr Pumprise

On the morning of 18 February, my 1986 Tarmak Shredar De Luxe was suddenly afflicted by a serious misfire as I was driving to my office. Since the car appeared to be on the brink of stalling, I was obliged to take it to the nearest garage.

Fortunately, or so I thought, the nearest garage was the Supafume Petroleum station at 534 Kamuter Street, Upper Ridges. I left my car with Mr Ridge, the owner, who promised to call me at my office as soon as he had diagnosed the problem. When I arrived at my office at eleven o'clock, there was no message from Mr Ridge, so I called him immediately. He informed me that the car needed a new fuel pump, which would be installed by the end of the day for a total price of £280.00.

Confident that a garage run by an organization of your reputation could be relied upon to perform a fair and workmanlike job, I authorized him to complete the work, and looked forward to collecting my car at the end of the day.

My confidence, however, was shattered by the size of the bill that greeted my arrival at the garage. Somehow, the £280.00 quote had grown to an astonishing £734.65! The £280.00 estimate for the fuel pump had increased to £295.00, which was reasonable. Mr Ridge's explanation for the additional £439.65 was, however, unacceptable. I was told that this was for an exchange carburettor, which was installed entirely without my knowledge or authority. The garage made no attempt to gain my authorization for the replacement carburettor.

It is odd that both the fuel pump and the carburettor should fail simultaneously, since these two parts function independently. However, the work has now been completed, and I am hardly in a position to verify the necessity of such an unexpected undertaking. The point remains that since I did not authorize the carburettor installation and was not given the option to refuse the extra work, I was certainly not prepared to pay the increased amount on the bill. Not surprisingly, I was not allowed to leave with my car until the full amount had been settled, which left me no choice but to pay up, despite my protests.

I am frankly appalled at this treatment, particularly since the Supafume impeccable reputation has always been upheld in my past experiences with your retail outlets. I would therefore be most grateful to receive your confirmation that this incident is not one that you are prepared to accept and that a refund of my £439.65 can be anticipated in the very near future.

I enclose for your information a photocopy of the invoice and credit card receipt for the job in question. I look forward to hearing from you.

Yours sincerely

Mustapha Nubike

Encl
cc Axel V Ridge, A V Ridge Wrench Auto

This letter should inspire the MD to investigate your complaint without delay, and you should be sent a reply confirming this.

Your letter has made it clear that you have a valid grievance, yet you have made no threats of legal recrimination, or forcefully demanded a refund. Instead you have given Supafume the opportunity to maintain their unblemished reputation and to retain you as a customer. You have made it clear that this is a matter of principle between two reputable parties, you and Supafume, and that you expect the refund just as soon as they have verified your claim.

If Supafume refuse to help you, then you will have to confront Mr Ridge's emporium directly. This could be a formidable challenge; you have discovered to your cost that A V Ridge is less than understanding. Since you have already dealt with the owner, there is no one with greater authority to turn to. None the less, it is not yet time to capitulate.

First, do a little research into the repair associations, motoring clubs, or similar organizations the garage claims to be affiliated with. The invoice and any notices inside or outside the garage may give you some clues, and your local library will be able to give you the names and addresses of consumer and business directories and guides in which the garage might be recommended. Compile a list of all these organizations, along with the name and title of whoever is in charge of them, and send them all copies of the letter you are now going to send Mr Ridge.

In particular, many reputable garages are members of the Retail Motor Industry Federation, the Society of Motor Manufacturers and Traders, or the Scottish Motor Traders Association. These bodies have a joint Code of Practice which their members must follow. The Code deals with repairs, servicing and handling complaints, and provides a low-cost arbitration procedure that can be used as an alternative to court action if you cannot get satisfaction. Copies of the Code can be obtained from any of these bodies.

Remember to send a copy of the letter to Supafume Petroleum. Never give up! Just because they claim they are not liable for any repair problems does not mean that you cannot continue to pressure them. They may still use their influence if you prove to be a serious nuisance!

If the garage was an independent, with no petrol outlet, this is also the letter you would have sent to the proprietor as your first step.

Mr Axel V Ridge, Proprietor
A V Ridge Wrench Auto
534 Kamuter Street
Upper Ridges
WE6 2GS

25 February 1993

Dear Mr Ridge

On the morning of 18 February, I brought my 1986 Tarmak Shredar De Luxe to your garage for attention to a misfire that had developed as I drove to work.

You explained that you could not immediately diagnose the problem, but you would examine the car later and phone me at my office with your verdict. Meanwhile, you insisted that I sign a blank work order, without which you said you had no authority to do any work on the car. Trusting that this was a mere formality, and since I had no alternative, I complied with your instructions and departed.

When I arrived at my office at eleven, there was no message from you, so I phoned you. You told me that my car needed a new fuel pump, which you could install by the end of the day for the inclusive price of £280.00. I gave you the authority to go ahead with the work.

When I arrived to pick up my vehicle, I was presented with a bill for £734.65, comprising £295.00 for the fuel pump and an additional £439.65 for a new carburettor, which was installed without my consent. I was quite prepared to pay the additional £15.00 for the fuel pump, since I accept that no estimate can be completely accurate, but I question the need for the new carburettor. I find it a remarkable coincidence that both the pump and carburettor failed simultaneously, since they work independently of each other.

You made no attempt to inform me of your decision to install the carburettor, despite my being at my telephone all day. You refused to discuss my concerns about this huge increase over your original agreed quotation, and told me that unless I paid in full, you would keep my car until the account was settled. Having no choice, I paid your account in full, under protest, and left with my car.

The fact remains, however, that you installed a carburettor without my knowlege or permission. Therefore, I require that my bill be reduced accordingly, and that you remit to me the sum of £439.65.

I expect to receive your cheque without delay.

Yours sincerely

Mustapha Nubike

cc Ryder Totruc, MD, Automotor Association
Ruth Less, MD, Retail Motor Industry Federation
Hy Pumprise, MD, Supafume Petroleum Ltd

A small business does not make as much profit as a large one, and may therefore be less willing, or able, to afford to give refunds. To win this one, you will need to be very determined and tenacious.

By sending the owner a letter that shows you have done your research and sent copies to organizations that might have some influence over him, or with whom he would like his reputation to remain unblemished, you show him that he must take you seriously. Although you are unlikely to receive any written response, there is a good chance that he may phone you to discuss a partial refund. The golden rule of not negotiating over the phone and insisting on written confirmation of any verbal promise may have to be broken in a case like this. Most small garages' expertise in correspondence is limited to handwritten estimates, signing for delivered parts, and writing up invoices. You will probably have to discuss the matter over the phone or at the garage. The phone is probably the safer option, if you want to avoid unhelpful pressure from the mechanics in attendance.

It is up to you whether to accept a partial refund. Keep in mind that your car has benefited from the new carburettor, despite your reluctance to pay for it. Had the garage called you and quoted you an additional £220.00 (half the amount you were charged) for a carburettor, you might have given them the authority to go ahead. And if you go to court, and the garage proves that a new carburettor was needed and that the failure to notify you of this prior to installing it was just an unintentional oversight, the judge may well decide that a fifty-fifty liability is appropriate.

Should you feel strongly that you will not settle for anything less than a full refund, then you will have to convince the garage owner that you are determined to do whatever is necessary to get your money back. You now visit your local small claims court to pick up some claim forms, which are free. The address of the court and be found under 'Courts' in the telephone directory.

At this stage, you are not going to file a claim, but you complete the form with the intention of issuing a summons if necessary. Whether you actually intend to take the matter to court is irrelevant at the moment. The object is to convince the garage that you do. To this end you must fill out the form with the details of the claim. (For more information about the small claims court and the form, see Chapter 10.) Make a photocopy to send with your letter.

You can now write your final letter to the garage, enclosing a copy of the claim form, which will carry a lot more weight than promises of legal action.

---

76 Drive Avenue
Lower Ridges
KW4 7ZR

Mr Axel V Ridge, Proprietor
A V Ridge Wrench Auto
534 Kamuter Street
Upper Ridges
WE6 2GS

20 March 1993

Dear Mr Ridge

Further to my claim for a refund of £439.65 charged by your garage on 18 February 1993, for the installation of a carburettor, without my knowledge or authorization, to my 1986 Tarmak Shredar De Luxe, as detailed in my letter of 25 February.

To date I have received no acknowledgment or offer in reply to my claim, and unless this amount is refunded in full by Wednesday, 3 April 1993, a summons will be issued with the court without further notice.

Prior to filing the claim, I enclose a copy for your information.

Yours sincerely

Mustapha Nubike

cc Ryder Totruc, MD, Automotor Association
Ruth Less, MD, Retail Motor Industry Federation
Hy Pumprise, MD, Supafume Petroleum Ltd

Copies of the letter should be sent to the associations listed in your letter, in order to further bring about a change of heart in Axel Ridge. Do not, however, include copies of the summons with the copy letters; send only the one to the garage. You have given notice that the claim will not be filed until 3 April; your circulating copies of the claim prematurely to parties who are not directly involved in the dispute could be interpreted as prejudice by your unreasonable anticipation of a negative response to your letter before the expiry of the advised deadline.

It is hoped that this final demand will convince Mr Ridge that to contest the matter further is not in his interest, and you will receive your refund within a couple of weeks. In any case, unless the garage is a member of a trade association, you will have exercised all the options available for settling the claim without resorting to court proceedings, and if you are out of luck, you can at least be satisfied that you did your best, or you can file the claim in court as promised.

Faulty repair job

It is wise to confirm the duration and extent of a guarantee for parts and labour before you give permission for any work to be done on your car. This is usually not done because you just want to know how much the repair will cost and when the car will be ready. Once the job is completed, you assume the repaired part will outlast the car, or last a reasonable time. Few garages give a separate guarantee, in addition to their normal invoice.

If you look at the back of the invoice, you may find a blanket warranty covering everything for a brief period or an equally unrealistic number of miles, 'whichever occurs first', and a disclaimer denying liability for secondary or consequential damages resulting from failure of the new parts or defective workmanship. The period is often expressed in days rather than months. Ninety days appears more reassuring than three months.

The mileage guarantee may be misleading. A 6,000 mile guarantee could expire after 60 days if you drive 100 miles a day. Some garages offer more realistic warranties, up to a year, or 12,000 miles which might appear reasonable, but in reality may be far from what should be expected.

For example, if you bought a new engine that failed at 13,000 miles, and the garage denied any liability because the warranty had expired, this would clearly be way below reasonable expectation for such a considerable outlay. The life expectancy of a car engine nowadays is more than 125,000 miles.

Even when a repair fails within the warranty period, you may be presented with a hefty bill for labour, since a 'parts only' clause is sometimes used. If a failed repair is put right by the garage responsible, and you are then given a bill for labour, you must refuse to accept liability for this arbitrary distinction. You have paid in good faith for a job that must have a reasonable life expectancy. If it does not meet these expectations, then the seller must do whatever is required to make good, entirely at his expense. There is no logic, and no legislation, that draws a line between materials and labour, yet garages occasionally practice this policy.

Garages cannot, legally or morally, decide on their own terms of liability to suit their individual business principles. The usual disclaimer in the warranty that absolves the garage from any liability arising from secondary or consequential damage resulting from defective parts or workmanship is deliberately intended to dissuade the customer from taking advantage of his legal entitlements. The garage cannot rely on such a disclaimer if it was not brought to your notice or displayed somewhere where you ought reasonably to have noticed it *before* you agreed to have the work done. Nor can the garage rely on it if it was so sweeping that it effectively tried to negate the garage's liability for the essential or fundamental part of the agreement. Nor can the garage rely on it if it was unfair to you.

The law implies certain terms into your contract with the garage which are designed to protect you, the consumer. The garage cannot avoid its liability under these laws by any means. The law says that all work done must be done with reasonable skill and care, at a reasonable price, within a reasonable time, and that any materials used will be of good quality and fit for their purpose. Garages which are members of the Retail Motor Industry Federation, the Society of Motor Manufacturers and Traders, the Scottish Motor Trade Association and the Vehicle Builders and Repairers Association must adhere to the codes of practice laid down by those bodies.

If, for example, you have a new set if tyres installed, and a couple of hours later one of your front wheels falls off because the mechanic forgot to tighten the wheel nuts, then the garage is entirely responsible for any and all claims that arise from the incident. Whatever the printed terms and conditions, they are entirely irrelevant, even if your signature shows your agreement with the terms.

Say the alternator on your 1988 Carnidge Extreme died seven months ago and was replaced for £325.23 at a local garage. At the time of the repair, you were told that you would also need a new voltage regulator because a malfunction of the alternator usually causes invisible damage to the regulator. Knowing that electricity can work in strange ways, you agree to both repairs.

Then, while driving home from work one day, you notice the ignition warning light is on, and pull over to investigate. A careful inspection under the bonnet reveals that nothing is obviously wrong, but the light refuses to go out. Clearly something is not right, and you decide to drive to the garage that installed the new alternator seven months ago.

Fortunately, the car makes it there. You describe the problem to the mechanic, explaining that the symptoms are the same as those that prompted the installation of a new alternator a few months back, and that you can scarcely believe that it has lasted for so short a time. The mechanic tells you to leave the car, which will be attended to first thing in the morning, and you catch a bus home, hoping for a quick and inexpensive solution. Before leaving, you note the reading on the odometer so that you can check how far you have travelled since the last repair, and it reads, 53,674 miles.

When you get home, you are relieved to discover that you still have the receipt for the origial repair, and that the odometer reading at the time was 42,432 miles. Grumbling that 12,000 miles of life is somewhat less than you were hoping for from the new parts, you turn to the back of the invoice to read the warranty. Less than reassuring, it states that the workmanship and parts installed are guaranteed for 26 weeks, or 10,000 miles, whichever occurs first. Needless to say, if it is necessary to produce the invoice in order to qualify for a free replacement, the service manager will be quick to point out that the warranty has expired, and that the garage is no longer responsible. Even though the warranty has expired, you still consider, but are not absolutely certain, that an alternator should last longer than seven months or 12,000 miles. You think the alternator was clearly not of good quality.

The next morning, feeling somewhat apprehensive, you call the garage and are told that the alternator is beyond repair and that it must be replaced.

There is no point in discussing the warranty at this stage, since the work will have to be done in any case, and it is in your interest to have it done as soon as possible. You therefore give the garage authority to go ahead, and do a little research in anticipation of any dispute that might ensue later. At least your car will be repaired and ready to go, no matter what transpires when you pick it up.

Assuming the worst, that the garage will indeed adhere rigidly to the conditions of its warranty, you should now phone two or three reputable repair shops in order to be able to present their guarantee conditions for comparison if need be. Phone a dealer (A) who specializes in your make of car, a garage (B) that does only auto-electrical repairs, and a large national garage chain (C). Ask them how much they charge for the same job, the length and type of their warranty, and also how long, in their professional opinion and experience, such a repair should be expected to last, notwithstanding any guarantee. Make careful notes of their answers. If necessary during your later negotiations, use only the answers that exceed your own expired warranty terms. Say, for example, A quotes a price of £368.00, with a warranty of 12 months or 20,000 miles, B charges £297.00 with a guarantee of 12 months or 18,000 miles and C wants £342.00 with a warranty of 12 months or 20,000 miles. And all three assure you that a new alternator should last for at least 50,000 miles. You are now certain that your alternator should have lasted longer and was therefore not of good quality.

Now you go to collect your car, taking your original invoice with you. The proprietor greets you with the job sheet covering your repair but, before he begins any calculations, you produce your bill and suggest firmly that since the original repair failed well before expectation, you do not expect to be charged for the job. Predictably, he examines the proffered bill in order to assess his liability. After a brief trip to confirm the reading on the odometer, he informs you that the warranty has expired, and that you will have to pay for the job in full.

This is where you introduce the terms under which his competitors do business. Don't arouse hostility by suggesting that his terms are deliberately set below acceptable levels, but name and quote the three installers you spoke to, and inform him that they all volunteered that you should have had 50,000 trouble-free miles from a new alternator. Point out that at the time of the original repair, you had no idea what the warranty comprised as you had not looked at the back of the invoice, and had naturally assumed that your repair should have lasted much longer.

Assure him that you have great faith in his ability and reputation, and because you assume that his workmanship and the quality of his parts are normally at least as good as those of his competitors, you find it strange that they offer better terms of satisfaction than his. Remind him that you prefer to use his garage for whatever reason you think is most appropriate and convincing. Perhaps he was recommended to you (name the person who made the recommendation if you can), or you and your family have always had excellent service in the past, or you know you can always rely on a smaller garage like his for personal and reliable attention. By appealing to his conscience, you hope that he will demonstrate he is willing and able to match the terms of his competitors.

Of course, you acknowledge that although he is legally responsible for the part failure, you realize he did not make the alternator and was just the unlucky recipient of a defective part. Cajoling him into the position of having to protect his reputation will be more productive than provoking an argument about his ability or integrity.

Your verbal strategy will be particularly effective if the discussion is held within earshot of employees or other customers. By matching his competitors' guarantees, he will demontrate his confidence in the performance of his garage. He would not want it understood that his questionable standard of service dictates a restricted warranty! If he stands his ground, then you will have to take steps similar to those described in the previous section.

Resist the temptation to turn the discussion into a vigorous argument, even if all your persuasive tactics fail. Instead pay the bill, remembering to mark the invoice and credit card receipt 'paid under protest', and remove your car from the premises.

If the garage is owned by, or conspicuously markets the products of, a major oil company, or is a dealership for a motor manufacturer or a distributor, then write to the MD of the company or the manufacturer's or the distributor's head office in the UK as follows:

---

56 Rectory Lane
Higher Meadows
YM5 2DT

Mr Lou Nattic, Managing Director
Liquid Petroleum Corporation plc
Liquid Centre
Bumetown
FG5 3EX

2 March 1993

Dear Mr Nattic

On 25 July 1992, I took my 1988 Carnidge Extreme to your garage located at 156 Green Street, Middle Meadows, to have a failed electrical system diagnosed and corrected. I was informed that I needed a new alternator, and was advised that the voltage regulator should be replaced at the same time because it would probably have been damaged by the failure of the alternator.

I agreed to have the work done, and paid the invoice for £325.23 on the understanding that I could now anticipate an extensive period of trouble-free driving. My expection was short lived, however, when after a mere 12,000 miles the new alternator failed completely on 26 February, and I was obliged to go back to your garage so that the repair could be made a second time.

To make matters worse, the proprietor, Mr A Paul Ling, refused to replace the faulty parts under warranty, and pointed out that the terms under which he operates limit the longevity of his workmanship to 10,000 miles, as stated inconspicuously on the back of his invoice. I informed Mr Ling that I had checked with three of his competitors and that they all had warranties for 1 year and/or 20,000 miles, but he was unimpressed and insisted that I pay for the job again or he would keep my car until the account was settled. Having no choice in the matter, I paid the £325.23 under protest, and removed my car from the premises. It is clear from what Mr Ling's competitors tell me, that the alternator Mr Ling supplied to me was not of good quality.

I am shocked to find that an organization of your reputation treats its regular customers with such minimal consideration, and I enclose copies of both invoices for your immediate attention.

Please let me know at your earliest convenience that you will be making a complete refund of the bill, dated 1 March 1993, and that a warranty more appropriate to the standards one might expect from the Liquid Petroleum Corporation plc will be given without delay.

Yours sincerely

Ray Vingmad

Encls
cc A Paul Ling, Porfix Garage Ltd

If the garage is controlled or owned by Liquid Petroleum, or the manufacturer or distributor, your letter should produce results. If, however, the company disclaims any liability on the grounds that Mr Ling is the MD of Porfix Garage Ltd, which is in no way connected to the company other than as a retailer of their petrol, cars and associated products, then, as in the preceding chapter, you will have to address the garage directly, as follows:

56 Rectory Lane
Higher Meadows
YM5 2DT

Mr A Paul Ling, MD
Porfix Garage Ltd
156 Green Street
Middle Meadows
YX4 7NB

9 March 1993

Dear Mr Ling

You will recall that on 26 February 1993, I brought my 1988 Carnidge Extreme to your garage because a warning light was on, indicating that the electrical system had failed.

As you had recently checked the system and installed a new alternator and voltage regulator, I brought the car to you again since it was possible that one of the new parts might need some minor adjustment. To my complete surprise, you told me that the alternator, newly installed 12,000 miles ago, had burnt out and that it would have to be replaced again, together with the regulator. Naturally, I had no choice but to agree to the replacement, but I assumed that since the original repair had lasted for such a short time, I would not be held responsible for further expense.

However, you presented me with another bill for £325.23, along with the explanation that the back of your original invoice described a warranty of only 10,000 miles. I voiced my opinion that this warranty had not been made clear to me at the time of the repair and that it was well below that expected from a garage with any confidence in the quality of its workmanship. I pointed out that three of your competitors back up their work with warranties for 1 year or 20,000 miles.

Nevertheless, you refused to negotiate, and I was obliged to pay you the full amount, under protest, in order to secure the release of my vehicle. Please note that I am convinced that your warranty is in no way appropriate to the repair in question, and that it is inferior to those given by your competitors and that the alternator you supplied to me was not of good quality as required by current consumer protection legislation.

Therefore I insist that my £325.23 be refunded at once and that your garage issue me a more comprehensive guarantee covering the work that was required after the premature failure of the first repair. Please note that I am prepared to take whatever steps are necessary to ensure that my money is refunded in full.

Yours sincerely

Ray Vingmad

cc Lou Nattic, MD, Liquid Petroleum Corporation plc
Ryder Totruc, MD, Automotor Association
Ruth Less, MD, Retail Motor Industry Federation

Again, you have done your homework, finding out the names of businesses or associations that might be unhappy to learn that their trading principles are under heavy attack, and you have sent their managing directors copies of the letter. You could also send a copy to the trading standards department at the local council that has jurisdiction over Mr Ling's particular business.

As I have described in the preceding section of this chapter, you may be offered a partial refund over the telephone. If that does not meet your requirements, then a final letter will have to be sent, again with a photocopy of a court summons, to show that you really do mean business.

---

56 Rectory Lane
Higher Meadows
YM5 2DT

Mr A Paul Ling, MD
Porfix Garage Ltd
156 Green Street
Middle Meadows
YX4 7NB

30 March 1993

Dear Mr Ling

I refer to my letter of 9 March 1993, requiring a refund of the £325.23 paid to your garage under protest on 27 February 1993, for the installation of an alternator and voltage regulator, replacing the units installed 12,000 miles previously which were not of good quality and not covered by adequate warranty.

Since you have not responded to my letter or settled my claim, please be aware that unless full payment is received by Monday, 13 April 1993, a court summons will be issued without further notice.

I enclose a copy of the claim for your information.

Yours sincerely

Ray Vingmad

Encl

cc Lou Nattic, MD, Liquid Petroleum Corporation plc
Ryder Totruc, MD, Automotor Association
Ruth Less, MD, Retail Motor Industry Federation

This should be more than enough to convince your opponent that he must take immediate action in order to protect his reputation and to forestall the summons. Unless he is convinced that your claim is unreasonable, a quick response can be anticipated. Again, if he offers a compromise payment, you will have to decide whether to accept. If you feel you must adhere to your principles and be paid in full, you can issue the summons as described in Chapter 10.

Used car is unroadworthy

Nothing presents a greater challenge than finding a used car that is in good condition and suits your budget. Besides the bewildering variety of makes, models and vintages, there are inexplicable differences in asking prices.

Logic would dictate that the higher the price, the better the quality, and that a car in exceptional condition will command a higher price than a particularly tired model of the same year. However, most sellers exaggerate the condition of the vehicle on offer and consequently inflate the price to match the described condition. The asking price is, therefore, not necessarily a reliable guide to the condition of a vehicle.

Before you embark on your search, you should ascertain the real market value of your intended purchase. There are monthly trade guides that list the wholesale and retail prices of virtually all makes and vintages available, and you should have this information before you start bargaining in earnest.

You will find all types of advertisers in your search: large dealers, who are usually dealers for a particular make but will sell other makes secondhand; much smaller 'back street' dealers, who offer a variety of different makes; and private individuals.

A reputable large dealer may appear to be the most reliable of the alternatives. If he is backed by one of the larger manufacturers, he will be mindful of their need to protect their reputation, and his performance will be geared accordingly. He will, presumably, be supported by the manufacturer he represents, a fact in your favour should you need to return a car for a subsequent repair. He will probably sell only recent models in good condition to protect his image. However, there are some disadvantages in buying from a large dealer: his prices are likely to be high; and bargaining for a discount may be a challenge if he is good shape financially and therefore in no hurry to sell. On balance, however, the big dealer is probably a good choice.

Should you not find what you want from a dealership, you might try the numerous back-street dealers, who usually have an extensive range of models, vintages and prices. Their overheads are lower than those of a large outlet, which is usually reflected in their prices, and they are invariably keen to make a sale, and will haggle for hours if they smell a positive outcome. This means that you can often bring down the price by a surprisingly large amount if you are unmoved by the dealer's pleas of poverty. There are possible drawbacks to keep in mind, too. In most cases, the smaller dealer has little knowledge of the history or condition of the vehicle up for sale; it was probably bought at auction, after little more than a brief inspection and a glance at the mileage, or bought from another dealer who felt it represented a risk. Often, a dealer does nothing but put the price on the windscreen, and only takes a closer look at the vehicle if a sale is conditional on an inspection.

Repairs are not always a dealer's business, and if the car you buy needs attention in order to pass MOT inspection, the dealer may require you to pay for the necessary repairs if you want an MOT. Of course, you may be fortunate enough to end up with a good car at a good price.

Another alternative is to buy from a private seller. You have the advantage of dealing with the owner rather than an agent. The owner best knows the reliability and general performance of his car, but you will have to decide whether the seller is honest. A test drive with an owner can reveal how the car has been treated. If the owner crunches the gears, screeches around corners, and constantly slams on the brakes you can safely deduce that the car has probably not enjoyed conditions conducive to a long life expectancy! With private sellers you can probably negotiate a considerable reduction in price: they are usually keen to make a quick sale, since selling through newspapers can be a trying business. So if you make a reasonable offer and produce a convincing wad of cash, you might have a deal.

But be aware that someone who appears at first sight to be a private seller in fact may be a trade dealer trying to pass himself off as a private seller. If he advertises goods for sale he must make it reasonably clear that he is doing so in the course of a business. It is a criminal offence not to do so. If your car subsequently goes wrong, the threat of reporting the dealer to the local Trading Standards Department will rapidly help him to see your point of view about repairs or a refund. A trade dealer will include someone who claims he does cars up 'as a weekend hobby'.

No matter where you buy your car, the seller is obliged to provide you with a vehicle that conforms to the description of its condition, whether verbal or written. Where the seller is a business, it must also ensure that it is suitable for the purpose for which it is intended, which means that it must be safe and roadworthy and that it is of merchantable quality.

There is no requiremnt that a used car should be sold with an MOT certificate. In practice, most reputable dealers will ensure the car has a valid MOT certificate. Dealers who are members of the Retail Motor Industry Federation, the Society of Motor Manufacturers and Traders and the Scottish Motor Trade Association are obliged by their joint Code of Practice to sell only cars that are roadworthy and have a valid MOT certificate.

It is a criminal offence to sell a car that is unroadworthy unless it is made clear to the buyer that the vehicle was only suitable for breaking up or in need of major repair. Unroadworthy means that the tyres, steering, brakes and so on are not up to the standards required by the law. The fact that a car has an MOT certificate is usually a good guide that the car is roadworthy but it does not guarantee it. Nor does the lack of an MOT certificate mean that it is unroadworthy.

So if you buy a car, you are entitled to assume that it is roadworthy unless you are told otherwise. If it turns out not to be roadworthy, the threat of reporting the seller to the local Trading Standards Department will undoubtedly facilitate a free repair or even your money back.

If you do have to report the seller to the Trading Standards Department and they subsequently prosecute him, you can ask the Department to ask the court to order the trader to pay compensation to you. The court does not have to do this and, if they do not, the fact that he has been convicted will greatly assist your own separate claim for compensation.

Let us assume that you have found the car you are looking for at a small back-street dealer who assures you that it is in excellent condition. After much haggling, you agree on a price, but when you request that the car be MOT'd, the dealer protests that since he let you have the car for such a generous discount, the cost of certification and any work necessary to bring it up to standard will have to be added to the purchase price. He pleads that any further expense, no matter how small, will mean a loss for him, and that since the car is obvously in good shape, you will easily be able to get it MOT'd yourself. Thus, swayed by your outstanding ability to outwit a professional car dealer at the negotiating game, and by sympathy for the unfortunate dealer, who seems like such a nice fellow, you agree to buy the car without an MOT. The dealer takes your money, gives you a receipt marked 'No warranty or MOT certificate – as is', together with the registration document and shakes your hand exuberantly while assuring you that the car will be no trouble at all. You drive your new machine happily off his premises and head for your local garage, which you have used for years and know to be honest and competent, to have the car MOT inspected.

Your mechanic is uncharacteristically quiet when you tell him how much you paid for the car, and tells you he will call you later in the day after he has given it a thorough inspection. Confident, you leave it with him, and go home to await the hour when you collect your freshly certified acquisition. When the phone rings at the end of the afternoon, you are somewhat surprised to learn that your mechanic wants you to drop by 'to go over a few problems'.

You head straight to the garage, where you are introduced to the underside of your car, which is hoisted for inspection. In shocked disbelief, you listed to a comprehensive list of serious faults: the chassis is badly rusted and requires extensive welding and new floor panels; two tyres need to be replaced; the silencer is leaking where it has been temporarily repaired with tape and putty; two ball joints on the front suspension are worn out; and both springs in the rear suspension are broken. Otherwise the car is fine!

Correcting these problems will cost £1,280.00, and the work will take four days to complete. There is some good news, however: the rest of the car is in good order, and when the repairs are done, you will be the owner of a car that meets your original expectation. These words of comfort do little to restore your faith in human nature. You paid £3,200.00 for the car, and for this together with the repair bill you could have bought a newer model.

You will now want to confront the dealer with a written estimate from your garage stating that the repairs are not merely cosmetic, that the vehicle is dangerous and undrivable, and that the work is the minimum required to make it roadworthy and to pass the MOT inspection. Include the cost of a hire or courtesy car, mileage charges and VAT in your estimate. You can now go back to the dealer and present your case. Phone first to make sure he will be there, and tell him a couple of problems have surfaced on which you would like his opinion.

Do not drive the car again in its present condition. Although the dealer is responsible for selling you an unfit vehicle, if you continue to use it and are stopped by the police, or have an accident, you may be held responsible for the consequences. If the dealer wishes to confirm the condition for himself, then he can visit the garage, pay to have it towed to his premises, or drive it back himself.

Before you confront the dealer, decide whether you want to keep the car and have it repaired at his expense, or whether you want a full refund. You might want to present him with the two alternatives and agree to accept the one he chooses, which will indicate some flexibility on your part, and may result in less hostility.

The dealer will undoubtedly produce his copy of the receipt and will insist that the disclaimer absolves him of any responsibility for what may be wrong with the car. You will have to convince him that you took him at his word when he told you the car was in good condition, and that you were entitled to assume the car was roadworthy, and that since he has been proved wrong, you have been misled, unintentionally or not. Besides which, you have been sold goods that are not in accordance with his description, or of merchantable quality and are not suitable for their intended purpose, and the 'as is' disclaimer cannot take away your legal rights.

You do now know how familiar the dealer is with his true legal position, but you can be sure that if he has been in business for some time, he knows from experience what he can get away with. You will have to make it clear that he has to choose one of the options you have given him, and that you are not prepared to compromise. Emphasize that you cannot drive the car because it is too dangerous for use on the public highway, and that he should go to the garage and see for himself. Offer to get a second opinion, if he doubts the validity of your estimate.

If all attempts to convince him that he has to meet your demands are met with absolute denial of responsibility, then you must tell him that you are not prepared to accept his protests, and that you will be informing him in writing immediately of the steps you are now obliged to take. You should then leave the dealer, decide which option is most acceptable to you, and write to the dealer with the details of what he must expect.

If you decide to return the car, you will be without transport again, and will probably have to pay to have the vehicle towed back to the dealer. It may take some time to recover the £3,200, and meanwhile you may have to spend at least the same amount again for a replacement. Also, as the £3,200 is over the limit for small claims, you will have to make your claim through the County Court. The latter is not as simple as small claims court, and you should check with the County Court in your area for the procedure for filing a claim. You may end having to use a solicitor to do this.

Although you will probably have to pay cash to the garage for the repairs, and it may be inconvenient to be out of pocket for a while, keeping the car is probably the better choice. You will not be without transportation since, while the repairs are being made, you will be using a hire car, and once the work is done, you will have the reliable vehicle you originally thought you were getting. You will save time searching for a replacement vehicle, and avoid the possibility of buying another 'surprise'. The amount you will be claiming is about £1,400.00 including the hire, but this amount is also above the limit of the small claims court. The dealer will be aware that he might have had to pay for the car to be repaired anyway in order to make a sale, in which case he is more likely to refund your £1,400 than he might have been to refund the full purchase price had you decided to return the car. Besides which, he may still make a profit – you do not know how little he paid for the car when he acquired it.

Assuming that verbal negotiation has proved fruitless and you have decided to keep the car, you authorize the garage to go ahead with the repairs (since correspondence will likely take a few days and you will be charged for storage if you leave the car untouched pending the outcome of your dispute). You rent alternative transport while the repairs are being done.

Now write to the dealer as follows:

---

23 Perrin Court
Long Acres
SW3 8TA

Mr Wat Arrek, Proprietor
Shay Dee Auto Sales
91 Sump Avenue
Long Acres SW5 5WR

3 March 1993

Dear Mr Arrek

On 29 February 1993, I purchased from your establishment, in good faith, a 1985 Ratling Titanic, serial number VVBTH4U6534R367, for £3,200.00, which I paid in cash.

You specifically described the car on several occasions during our negotiations as being in good condition, trouble free, and in excellent shape. Having no reason to doubt your word, and relying on your expertise in such matters, I was convinced by your confidence and agreed to purchase the car. In order to ensure that the vehicle was legally roadworthy, I requested that you have the car inspected and MOT certified.

You were reluctant to do this, and explained that I would have to pay extra for what I assumed should have been a routine procedure. However, you assured me that the vehicle would pass inspection without any problems, and so I took your word and concluded our transaction accordingly.

I then drove the car to a garage which does MOTs. The Injerd Auto Garage Ltd, 12 Main Street, Long Acres, where the owner, Mr Miles Perower, agreed to perform the required checks. Some hours later, Mr Perower informed me that the car had failed the inspection for several reasons, and I was shocked to learn of the following serious problems:

- Badly rusted chassis, requiring extensive welding and new floor panels
- Two cut tyres needing replacement
- A temporarily repaired silencer needing replacement
- Two ball joints on the front suspension worn out
- Both rear suspension springs broken.

The cost for repairing these defects in order to make the car legally roadworthy is £1,280.00, plus £115.00 for a hire car for four days during the work, a total of £1,395.00. Mr Perower also advised that, because the vehicle is in such a dangerous condition, I should not drive it until all these faults had been corrected.

On 2 March 1993, I presented you with these facts and, since you had sold me a vehicle that was not in accordance with your description, was not of merchantable quality and was totally unsuitable for the purpose for which it was intended, in contravention of consumer protection legislation, and that it was unroadworthy, I requested that the vehicle be repaired at your expense, or that the purchase price be refunded in full.

You refused on the grounds that the vehicle was bought 'as is' and so you were not responsible for its condition once it left your premises. Despite your protest, I hold you entirely responsible for selling me a vehicle that failed to meet its advertised description and the legal safety requirements, and which was not of merchantable quality or fit for its purpose.

I have authorized The Injerd Auto Garage Ltd to begin the necessary repairs at once, and I look to you for the immediate settlement of their account, which totals £1,395.00. Kindly forward to my address your remittance for this amount without delay. If you fail to do so, further steps wil be taken to ensure collection.

Yours sincerely

Sue Togetrich

Encl
cc Lisa Lorry, Trading Standards Dept, Long Acres Council
Phil Estein, MD, Retail Motor Industry Federation

As I have explained earlier in this chapter, you will have to do a little homework to discover the organizations to whom copies of your letter should be sent. If the dealer doesn't respond, or offers a partial settlement that is unacceptable, you will have to send a final demand, with a photocopy of a completed summons, as described in a previous example and in Chapter 10. Write as follows:

---

23 Perrin Court
Long Acres
SW3 8TA

Mr Wat Arrek, Proprietor
Shay Dee Auto Sales
91 Sump Avenue
Long Acres
SW5 5NR

18 March 1993

Dear Mr Arrek

To date, I have received no response to my letter of 3 March 1993, requiring you to pay for the essential repairs to the dangerous and unroadworthy 1985 Ratling Titanic you sold me on 29 February 1993.

Repairs have now been completed to my satisfaction, and the car has passed the required MOT inspection. Enclosed is the invoice for the necessary repairs and the hire car, totalling £1,395.00, as per the estimate in my previous letter.

Please note that unless this amount is received by me in full by Thursday, 2 April 1993, a summons will be issued without further notice. For your information, I enclose a copy of the summons.

Perhaps I may expect to hear from you before 2 April?

Yours sincerely

Sue Togetrich

Encls
cc Lisa Lorry, Trading Standards Dept, Long Acres Council
Phil Estein, MD, Retail Motor Industry Federation

Remember to send each party a copy of the letter only, not a copy of the summons.

The dealer should now clearly understand your determination to pursue your claim through all means at your disposal, and should be quite shaken by your quick action and tenacity. It is entirely possible that in his line of work, he is obliged to spend considerable time defending his reputation! The spectre of a court appearance may unsettle him and you may receive an acceptable offer well before you have to file the claim. If further action is necessary, you should have all the evidence you need to prove your claim.

New car is a disaster

Most motorists spend their first few years on the road driving a variety of used cars. Ancient and weary cars exhaust their impoverished owners with their quirks and their unfailing tendency to expire whenever overstretched budgets can least accommodate any more endurance tests. What great joy, then, when after years of hard work and a successful campaign to deceive your bank, you arrange the financing of your first brand-new car, and banish the dark memories of constant breakdowns to the dim pages of never-to-be-repeated history.

Unfortunately, new cars can be as much trouble as used ones, especially mass-produced vehicles at the lower end of the price range. Manufacturers, in order to increase profits and stay competitive, pare the quality of the components down to the absolute minimum specification required to do a particular job and to last only for the duration of the warranty. If the engineers and accountants have combined their talents on a particular model, there are sure to be shortcomings in quality. These faults will inevitably appear and should be covered by the manufacturer's warranties.

The dealership and the manufacturer are entirely responsible for any defects that occur through no fault of your own. Should your new car display unwanted quirks, you must make your displeasure very clear. Any inconvenience or expenses you suffer as a result of these shortcomings should be kept to an absolute minimum. Conversely, any inconvenience or expenses to the dealer and manufacturer should be maximized! This will increase their motivation to turn you into a satisfied customer as soon as possible.

Don't let dealers and manufacturers dictate their terms to you. If you purchase a vehicle with a guarantee of three years and a life expectancy of ten years, you have every right to expect it to perform accordingly.

If you will accept a repair, unless the repair can be fixed on the spot and quickly, you are entitled to alternative transportation. If the dealer does not have a courtesy car or is not willing to provide one, you must hire one and invoice the dealer. In fact, you can give the dealer several options if taking your car into the dealership disrupts your working day. He can arrange to have your car picked up and have a courtesy car left for you, or you will hire one yourself. He can stay open until you are able to deliver the car after work, or you will deliver it during your working day, and invoice him for the inconvenience and loss of income in addition to any hire charges. After a demonstration of your technique, you will find him very keen indeed to make sure your car runs as smoothly as possible.

Don't allow the dealer to sway you with smooth assurances that the warranty doesn't cover hire cars, customer inconvenience and expenses, labour charges, or whatever else. If a part under warranty expires, its replacement must be covered, including labour. Had the part been adequately manufactured and installed in the first place, as should be expected in a new car, you would be happily driving the car instead of spending your valuable time in a repair shop.

Don't feel sorry for the salesman because he was so kind and helpful when you bought the car. All salesmen are kind and helpful – that is how they are able to sell things! Everyone leaves car showrooms wondering whether to invite the salesman over for dinner to celebrate their new friendship, while back in his office, the salesman is gleefully patting himself on the back for having converted another hesitant and trusting customer into a commission!

And don't feel guilty because it's not the dealer's fault if the manufacturer sends him an occasional dud. No one forced him to be a dealer for that particular manufacturer. He is an expert on the makes he sells, and knows exactly how good or bad they are; he earns a great deal of money on every new vehicle he sells; and he, in turn, will be claiming his losses for repairs back from the makers. And he will be keeping his mechanics gainfully employed!

Let's say that, while driving along to work one fine day, your GT 4000 backfires, gives a shudder, and dies on the road. You call the dealer, but there is no reply. So you leave a conspicuous note on the dashboard explaining that the car has broken down and is awaiting a tow, leave a spare key in the glove compartment, make sure the car is fully locked, and take the most convenient method of transport to work. If you take a taxi, don't forget to get a receipt from the driver.

When you arrive at work, you call the dealer again, and after explaining the events of the morning and where the car is, you ask him whether he will pick it up, or whether he would prefer you to make the arrangements and invoice him later. He tells you that he cannot provide a courtesy car unless he is given adequate notice, and that all his cars are in use. You repeat that you need a replacement car immediately, that you will hire one yourself, and present him with the bill as soon as your own car is satisfactorily repaired and returned. Remember to speak to the person with the highest authority – the MD will do fine.

Having made your course of action perfectly clear, you then hire your replacement, and continue to use it until the dealer tells you that own car is ready. It is up to the dealer to let you know when it is ready, but the longer it takes the dealer to repair your car, the greater will be his expense for a hire car. In this case your car is ready three days later. You should prepare an invoice, including all reasonable expenses, that should look like the specimen over the page.

Rick Shaw
32 Chalk Road
Redemption
TT4 4FP

Mr Austin Tashous, MD
Dume & Gloume Auto Sales Ltd
10 Cruquide Avenue
Redemption
TT2 9PQ

28 February 1993

INVOICE

Re: Armageddon Perrish 4000 GT Serial number 564679876BW5634DQ78, purchased new on 15 January 1993.

For expenses incurred as a result of deprivation of use of the above vehicle from 8:12 am on 25 February 1993, to 7:00 pm on 28 February 1993, as a result of premature failure and subsequent replacement and repair of electrical wiring to distributor. Repaired under 36-month warranty.

Taxi from breakdown site 25 February to workplace	£8.27
Loss of wages 25 February, ¾ hour @ £28.50 per hour	£21.37
Hire car from 25 February to 28 February (copy invoice enclosed)	£125.87
Total this invoice	£155.51

Terms: Net monthly. Overdue accounts attract interest at 1.5% per month.

When you meet Mr Tashous, or a colleague with the authority to make decisions, point out firmly and calmly that since the warranty covers the cost of replacing any faulty parts, it must also cover all damages resulting from the defect. Be clear that you are not going to back away from or reduce your claim, and ask him to authorize the payment. If he does not immediately reach for the Dume & Gloume chequebook, inform him that you will be including the unpaid invoice, together with a covering letter detailing your continuing disappointment in their products and service, to Armageddon Motors.

The next step is a letter to the MD of Armageddon Motors, as follows:

---

32 Chalk Road
Redemption
TT4 4FP

Mr Gerry Attrick, MD
Armageddon Motors Ltd
Great Bolzup
Motoun
MR4 7SL

29 February 1993

Dear Mr Attrick

I was so impressed by your many lavish and persuasive television and newspaper advertisements highlighting the performance and innumerable virtues of the Armageddon Perrish 4000 GT, that I was convinced this must be car to fulfil all my needs, and on 15 January 1993, I purchased a brand-new model from your authorized dealer, Dume & Gloume Auto Sales Ltd, in Redemption.

The full purchase price of the car was £23,673.34, and for this not inconsiderable sum, I confidently anticipated that I might have several years of comprehensively warrantied, trouble-free motoring, as strongly emphasized in your advertising and confirmed in glowing terms by your representatives at Dume & Gloume Auto Sales. As a fellow businessman, I know you will appreciate my extreme disappointment and annoyance when my Perrish broke down at an extremely inconvenient moment in my working week, after less than two months. This is hardly a glowing testimony to the accuracy of your advertising.

The necessary repairs have now been completed, and in view of this alarming example of premature mechanical fragility, I would be very keen indeed to receive your considered estimate of how often I am likely to experience further lamentable demonstrations of such unreliability. I would also appreciate your immediate settlement of the enclosed invoice for £155.51, covering my losses resulting from the breakdown.

Since the warranty covers all faults that arise as a consequence of faulty or defective parts or workmanship, it must, therefore, also include losses as a result of such failures incurred by the owner of the warranty. Messrs Dume & Gloume have failed to grasp this important point, and I would be most grateful for your speedy remittance.

I look forward to your early reply, and settlement of my invoice.

Yours sincerely

Rick Shaw

Encl
cc Austin Tashous, MD, Dume & Gloume Auto Sales Ltd

You send a copy to Mr Tashous in the hope that he may be frightened into sending you a cheque and his abject apology at once. Furthermore, it is good manners to keep him informed of your persistence and your lack of tolerance of shoddy treatment.

A reply may not be immediate, for there will undoubtedly be some discussion between the manufacturer and the dealer before a decision can be arrived at, and acted upon.

If you have not received any response in say, ten days, a gentle reminder to the chairman should keep the ball rolling, and will keep you from getting too bored! Something along these lines should suffice:

---

32 Chalk Road
Redemption
TT4 4FP

Mr Cy Lynderhead, Chairman
Armageddon Motors Ltd
Great Bolzup
Motoun
MR4 7SL

9 March 1993

Dear Mr Lynderhead

On 28 February, I was obliged to write to your MD, Gerry Attrick, concerning the appalling reliability of my new automobile manufactured by your company, and the consequent distress and financial loss I have suffered through this experience.

Thus far, Mr Attrick has not seen fit to address my concerns, and I would be obliged if you could ensure that either he or his successor takes immediate steps to settle this outstanding matter. Please let me know by return post that you have personally taken charge of this unfortunate incident, and that it will be resolved to my satisfaction without delay.

Thank you in anticipation.

Yours sincerely

Rick Shaw

Note that you have deliberately given as few details of your complaint as possible. This means that Mr Lynderhead will have to interrupt his busy schedule to get a copy of your letter from his MD in order to understand the nature of the problem. The MD should then be quite keen to settle with you, and a quick response can be anticipated.

You will also have noted that a copy of this letter was not sent to the dealer. You don't want the dealer to know that your letter to the MD went unanswered. In the remote possibility that your latest letter goes unanswered, too, then a final letter will be sent to the MDs of both the dealership and the manufacturer as follows:

Mr Austin Tashous, MD
Dume & Gloume Auto Sales Ltd
10 Cruquide Avenue
Redemption
TT2 9PQ

& Mr Gerry Attrick, MD
Armageddon Motors Ltd
Great Bolzup
Motoun
MR4 7SL

18 March 1993

Dear Sirs

To date, my invoice of 28 February 1993, for £155.51, remains unpaid.

Your failure to accept responsibility for losses arising from the sale of faulty and unreliable goods is both deplorable and unacceptable, and will not be tolerated.

Unless full settlement is received by Monday, 13 April 1993, a summons will be issued against both Dume & Gloume Auto Sales Ltd and Armageddon Motors Ltd without further notice.

Yours sincerely

Rick Shaw

This should finally sway them, since a court appearance will be time consuming for both defendants, and the potential bad publicity most undesirable. If issuing the summons becomes necessary, details of the appropriate procedure is covered in Chapter 10.

If, as is most likely, your invoice is paid with little protest by either the maker or the dealer, or the amount is paid into court, or the court rules against the defendants, you will have established a precedent, which can be cited to expedite any further claims should your car continue to perform unreliably.

If the manufacturer and the dealer still remain stubborn and refuse to meet your claim, now would be the time to involve the trade associations and the Trading Standards Department of the local authority in which the dealer is situated. The dealer and the manufacturer are both likely to be members of one or more of the Retail Motor Industry Federation, the Society of Motor Manufacturers and Traders and the Scottish Motor Trade Association. These three bodies have jointly published a Code of Practice to which its members must adhere. The Code provides a complaint handling and arbitration procedure, which can be used as an alternative or as a preliminary to court action.

If your car is repeatedly unreliable, you might consider demanding a complete refund of the purchase price, though you will by now have lost your legal right to a refund. Nevertheless, it is worth a go. If you want to take such drastic action, having written evidence for all repairs and collecting compensation for financial losses incurred will be to your advantage. The dealer may be quite amenable to negotiating a reimbursement if he weighs it against the continuing expense and inconvenience of dealing with you. He already knows that your demands cannot be treated lightly.

If you do decide that enough is enough, that you are fed up watching your vehicle heading off into the sunset attached to the business end of a tow truck, then you must collect all your evidence, and arrange to meet Mr Tashous. By now you should know him quite well, so a verbal discussion is quite in order and, if conducted civilly, will not prejudice any further written exchange that may be required. Arrange all your invoices and expenses in chronological order, and then list them on a separate sheet of paper, totalling the various inconveniences under appropriate sub-headings, including the approximate cost of each repair had it not been completed under warranty. This will emphasize the amount of money that Dume & Gloume or the manufacturer is losing by keeping the vehicle on the road.

Make the list look comprehensive and professional – it may need to be used in court.

Record of repairs to Armageddon Perrish 4000 GT, Chassis Number 56467876BW5634DQ78, purchased new on 15 January 1993, from Dume & Gloume Auto Sales Ltd by Rick Shaw.

31 July 1993

Date & Repair	*Cost of Repairs*	*Expenses Paid to Owner*
28 February 1993 New BotchAmp electronic management system, and distributor wiring	£973.00	£155.51
14 April 1993 New transmission	£1,536.00	£203.65
4 May 1993 New power steering	£1,134.00	£101.54
etc.		
7 breakdowns/repairs	£6,342.00	£873.89
Total cost	£7,215.89	

Present the list and suggest that the theoretical costs of running the car so far amount to £13,321.64 annually. Mention that you sympathize with Mr Tashous's position, of course, and confirm that you appreciate the cooperation and service he has provided over the months but, despite the friendship that has built up through your frequent visits to his establishment, you must insist that you be relieved of the burden of owning the recalcitrant vehicle. As a demonstration of your unflagging devotion to fair-mindedness and flexibility, offer him a choice of how to refund your money. Your preference would be for the dealership to give you a complete refund of the purchase price. Or, if this is not convenient, you will sell the car yourself, and look to the dealer for the difference between the original price paid and the amount realized from the secondhand sale, plus any additional expenses incurred for advertising the car.

Of course, it is only fair to mention that, should you have to sell the car yourself, as an honest and considerate person, you will be under a moral and legal obligation to accurately describe to potential buyers the problems you have experienced during your ownership.

You should find the dealer most cooperative, but he will probably not want to seem too eager to capitulate. You may need to let him think it over for a day or two. He will by then have weighed the situation carefully, and have consulted with the manufacturer. Should he not be persuaded by your argument, then you will have to confirm your intentions in a letter to both the dealer and the manufacturer as follows:

---

32 Chalk Road
Redemption
TT4 4FP

Mr Austin Tashous, MD	&	Mr Gerry Attrick, MD
Dume & Gloume Auto Sales Ltd		Armageddon Motors Ltd
10 Cruquide Avenue		Great Bolzup
Redemption		Motoun
TT2 9PQ		MR4 7SL

4 August 1993

Dear Sirs

Further to my conversation with Mr Austin Tashous on Friday, 31 July 1993 concerning the continuing lack of reliability of my Armageddon Perrish 4000 GT, serial number 56467876BW5634DQ78, purchased on 15 January 1993, from Dume & Gloume Auto Sales Ltd, I confirm herewith that I am no longer prepared to endure the unacceptable burden of ownership of this vehicle.

Enclosed is a list of the faults that have plagued the car from the time of purchase to the present date, which is excessive for any form of transport, let alone a car that was purchased brand-new.

Should the unreliability continue at its present rate, the cost of repairs and resulting expenses will amount to £13,321.64 per annum. Furthermore, my daughter will be using the car to drive to her new job, which is some distance out of town, and I am not prepared to risk her safety should the car break down at night or far from assistance. Any additional expenses incurred through hiring a replacement vehicle and repairs by a local garage, if required, would considerably increase the estimate described above.

Kindly confirm, therefore, that you will make the necessary arrangements to cancel my purchase contract, take back the car, and refund in full the purchase price of £23,673.34 without delay.

In the event that you are not prepared to comply with my claim, please be advised that I will have no alternative but to sell the vehicle myself and look to you for the difference between the amount realized and the original purchase price. My legal and moral obligation to disclose the number and frequency of repairs experienced to date to any prospective purchaser will no doubt adversely influence the price the car might sell for, which will be reflected in the balance I shall be seeking in compensation.

I look forward to your immediate proposals.

Yours sincerely

Rick Shaw

Encl

If neither of your proposals is accepted, you will have to decide which option is most convenient and give the manufacturer and dealer final notice of your intention. Incidentally, if you are still making monthly payments on the car, don't be tempted to stop the payments – apart from the risk of repossession, your wanting to return the car could be interpreted as your inability to make payments. If you have decided to return the car rather than sell it, write a final letter as follows:

---

32 Chalk Road
Redemption
TT4 4FP

Mr Austin Tashous, MD
Dume & Gloume Auto Sales Ltd
10 Cruiquide Avenue
Redemption
TT2 9PG

& Mr Gerry Attrrick, MD
Armageddon Motors Ltd
Great Bolzup
Motoun
MR4 7SL

13 August 1993

Dear Sirs

Further to my letter dated 4 August 1993, in which I gave notice that my 1993 Armageddon Perrish 4000 GT was so appallingly unreliable that I had no option but to return it for complete reimbursement of the purchase price of £23,673.34.

I am disappointed to learn that you are not prepared to take back the car and refund my money. I must therefore inform you that in order to satisfy my claim, a summons for the full amount plus costs will be issued without further notice, unless full settlement is received by Monday, 7 September 1993.

I am sure you are aware that the publicity generated by this action could affect future sales. I trust you share my interest in ensuring that any such publicity does not become necessary, and look forward to your taking appropriate preventive measures before the above date.

I shall maintain possession of the vehicle in question pending the decision of the court.

Yours sincerely

Rich Shaw

cc Cy Lynderhead, Chairman, Armageddon Motors Ltd

Sending a copy to the chairman will ensure that all parties are aware of what is about to be initiated and have the opportunity to pre-empt your action.

This is as far as you can reasonably take this threat. You will by now have lost your legal right to a refund of the purchase price, so you should not actually issue your threatened summons. But it may produce some compensation from the dealer or the manufacturer.

4

Till Death Do Us Part: Insurance Woes

Insurance is a reluctant necessity, and even if you are fortunate enough to live from cradle to grave without making a claim, the premiums are gone forever!

Unjustified rate increase

Insurance renewal time is rarely an occasion for hilarity and spontaneous celebration: premiums increase with monotonous regularity, usually with no explanation or justification. If you have an excellent claim record, which logic would dictate should result in a *reduction* in premiums, this can be very irritating. Unfortunately, your unblemished record generally fails to impress those responsible for deciding how much you can afford to pay! A slight increase over the rate of inflation can be justified, and sometimes even a large increase; you might, for instance, own a rare car that has increased sharply in value over the past year. On the other hand, if your premium is substantially higher for no apparent reason, you should seek a reduction.

Insurers and brokers make it their business to know the value of the goods they insure: you should make it yours, too. A diligent insurer will be aware of any factors that could affect your premiums: a sharp increase in burglaries in your neighbourhood or a new railway line that could pose a potential hazard. An increase in property value, due to high demand, however, should not affect premiums since the cost of repairs does not change even if the land value does rise. New risks do justify a higher rate, but you should ensure that any increase is applied only to that portion of the policy to which it is applicable. For instance, a 15 per cent increase in break-ins in your town over the last year should mean that only the theft portion of your home insurance should be increased 15 per cent.

Insurance is generally purchased through independent brokers, and renewal notices from your broker are usually accompanied by a letter stating that the new premiums were compared with those offered by alternative companies and were found to be competitive. This may be true, but you are hardly in a position to judge. It is unlikely that a broker would have the time to compare premiums every time a policy is due for renewal. Therefore you should compare your rates with at least one other broker or insurance company each year. Your savings may be substantial.

Let us assume that you live in a modest block of flats in a thriving and industrious city, and that you regularly insure the contents of your flat, which includes such items as a television and VCR, a microwave oven, and some jewellery bequeathed by a departed aunt. You have been insured by the same company for seven years, through a local broker, and have never made a claim of any kind. Last year the premium was assessed at £211.67, and the year before it was £192.84. The increase was certainly in excess of inflation, but still reasonable.

This year, the renewal notice arrives ten weeks before the due date so that the insurance company can have your money in its possession for as long as possible. (And it works! Most customers pay quickly 'just to be on the safe side'.) The premium is £253.78, or up more than 20 per cent over last year, with no explanation whatsoever from the broker or the principal. You are surprised since you have not made a claim or altered the terms of coverage in any way. So what should you do?

Initially, a call to the broker will do no harm and might well result in an immediate, satisfactory explanation. However, in this case your agent tries to placate you with bland and imprecise reasons for the high premium, which include an increased number of claims, the high cost of replacing stolen or damaged goods, the escalation of crime in inner cities, and so forth. Naturally, you are not impressed since the broker is unable to furnish any viable statistics that might give the increase some credibility. The agent assures you that the premium is still competitive and that rates have gone up throughout the insurance industry for the reasons just offered.

This explanation is unsatisfactory and clearly demonstrates which client is more important to the agent: the insurance company. Having learned little from the broker, you should now confront the insurers directly. But before doing so, give the broker the benefit of the doubt, and phone two other agencies for quotes, just in case all insurance companies have indeed put up their rates.

A few telephone calls later, you have quotes for identical insurance that range from £182.75 to £215.00. At this stage, you could switch your business to a new company, but you might want to stay with your present insurers because they are particularly reputable when it comes to settling claims. Better the devil you know . . .

The renewal date is still several weeks ahead, so you have plenty of time to decide. Meanwhile you could discover that your present company had made a 'mistake', if pressed with sufficient conviction! However, it is vital to handle the dispute in a businesslike manner, and to maintain existing insurance or commence consecutive new insurance. Insurers cannot be relied upon to continue extended coverage while money is owed on unpaid premiums, even while a difference of opinion is under negotiation. And the insurer, who is always firmly on top of matters, could notify you that your policy has been cancelled.

In this case, armed with the knowledge that lower rates are readily available elsewhere, it is time to convey your reluctance to pay more than necessary to your insurer as follows:

Flat 403
11 Steel Avenue
Mediocher City
AX5 2AT

Mr Robin Pillidge, MD
Graspp Fearcely Insurance Ltd
Babel Towers
Gratinkum
RU4 0LT

4 October 1993

Dear Mr Pillidge,

I have been privileged to enjoy insurance coverage (Policy No GFI 3478623/6478) provided by your company for seven years, and purchased through your agents, Messrs Harp, Gripe & Mone Insurance Brokers Ltd, of 43 Titannic Street, Mediocher City. During this time, I have always received courteous and efficient service from both you and your agents, and have been pleased with the competitive rates offered.

I was therefore surprised and shocked to see that my new premium has been increased by 20 per cent, to £253.78, with no explanation for this unexpectedly high amount.

My records will show that I have never made a claim of any kind, that my status has not altered since beginning coverage seven years ago, and that I have always paid due premiums on demand.

I called my representative at Harp, Gripe & Mone, Mr Harry Hopelis, who offered various vague possibilities by way of an explanation, none of which appeared to carry much conviction. Mr. Hopelis assured me that the new premium was still competitive. In order to verify his statement, I checked with some of your competitors. All five quotations were considerably less than the new premium required by your organization, and in fact, two of the quotes were for less than last year's premium!

I can only assume, therefore, that an error has occurred in the assessment of my new premium, and I should be most grateful if you could look into this at once, and let me know the correct amount at your earliest convenience.

In view of our mutually compatible relationship over the past seven years, I am naturally anxious it should continue uninterrupted, and I feel sure you would not want my business to be given to any of the several competitors who are apparently keen to offer a more attractive proposition than your own good organization.

I look forward to receiving details of my revised premium soon, and thank you in anticipation.

Yours sincerely

Joan Ovvark

cc Harp, Gripe & Mone

A copy of the letter was sent to the brokers as a courtesy, and to indicate to them that their performance has scarcely created a favourable impression.

Note that, in order to avoid leading the insurer into what could be a protracted and complex analysis of crime statistics, inflation's effect on the cost of damage repairs and so forth, no request for the reasons for the increase has been made. This way you avoid having to dispute those parts of the explanation you disagree with. Instead, you are merely pointing out to the insurer that his rates are seriously out of line with the competition's and that, if he wants to keep your patronage, he now has the opportunity to appease you by correcting an unfortunate miscalculation by one of his subordinates. If he does reduce the premium, the exercise will have been successful with very little exertion from you.

On the other hand, the insurer may provide a logical explanation for the increase, and you will achieve little through further correspondence. Since better rates are available and since initiating a new policy is a fairly painless operation, you would then be well advised to take your business elsewhere.

However, a parting shot will do no harm, and just might result in a change of heart or change of policy, if I may be allowed an unintentional pun! A final letter, such as the one following, will inform the insurance company that its rates are responsible for losing your valuable custom. If enough clients voice their opinion, perhaps the company will take notice, which will at least benefit future customers.

Flat 403
11 Steel Avenue
Mediocher City
AX5 2AT

Mr Robin Pillidge, MD
Graspp Fearcely Insurance Ltd
Babel Towers
Gratinkum
RU4 0LT

24 October 1993

Dear Mr Pillidge,

I have received your letter dated 22 October, replying to my request for the premium on my insurance policy number GFI 3478623/6478 to be reduced to a realistic level.

I have read your reasons for justifying such an exorbitant increase, and I am unable to accept your explanation.

Kindly be aware, therefore, that as of the expiry date of my policy, 31 December 1993, I shall be insuring with one of your numerous competitors, who is still able to offer coverage at reasonable and competitive rates.

Yours sincerely

Joan Ovvark

cc Harp, Gripe & Mone

Realistically, this is probably the best that can be done. Whatever the outcome, you are in a position to obtain a lower insurance rate.

Property damage not covered

The most valuable item the majority of people will ever insure is their home. But a house can be a complex and demanding possession, and the owner will undoubtedly be liable for a plethora of problems and repairs.

Comprehensive insurance coverage is essential, and great care must be taken to ensure that your policy specifically covers the property for all the eventualities that might befall it – exclusions or vague definitions can be ruinously expensive. Read your policy carefully, and make a note of anything you don't understand. Insurance terminology is geared, accidentally or deliberately, to completely baffle the insured, and it is usually no challenge to find clauses that are vague, contradictory, or open to subjective interpretation.

Insurance policies are interpreted very strictly. The benefit of the doubt is never given to the policyholder. So you need to make absolutely sure that you really are covered for the risks you think you are covered for.

You should make a list of all the eventualities that need to be covered, and have your insurer or broker tailor a policy to your needs. Since even made-to-measure policies are likely to contain vague clauses, before signing or accepting the document, you might also request a covering letter that itemizes your requirements and confirms where each item is included in the policy if you are in any doubt. It is usually the case that if a particular hazard is not included in the policy, then it will not be covered. So check carefully.

As you make your list, walk around your house and grounds, noting all the accidents and incidents that might happen over a lifetime. Don't leave out anything, no matter how bizarre or unlikely. Use a fresh page for each of the seasons; every season has its potential hazards, and unless you specifically think yourself into the appropriate time of year, you may miss a necessary item. On a hot August day, for instance, you might forget that your roof could cave in during an unexpectedly heavy snowfall in the middle of a January night, or that your basement could be flooded during a spring thaw.

Imagine the reasons your insurer might cite for refusing to pay a claim. Suppose your postman steps on a loose or rotten tread on your front steps and is injured: the insurer might claim that you were negligent in maintaining your property and deny any liability. But what if the step had rotted from underneath, where water had been trapped between the tread and the stringer, out of sight and quite unknown to you? Would this still be interpreted as improper maintenance? Or suppose the postman was injured on your property by a brick falling from a chimney on the house next door. Your neighbours have no insurance, and dispute their liability because the postman was not on their property. Would your coverage be sufficient to indemnify you?

Or perhaps you and your family decide to visit relatives in Australia, and in view of the distance and expense, opt to make a marathon of it and stay for three months. In order to defray your daunting expenses, you rent the house while you are absent to a neighbour's relatives who happen to be on an extended visit to your town. If they accidentally flood the basement, causing considerable damage, will the insurers reject your claim because your coverage is for a private residence and not a rented property?

The possibility of any accident or loss, no matter how unlikely, should not be overlooked. Like any other business, an insurance company operates to make a profit, and even the most reputable organization may refuse to honour a claim if in its opinion the policy holder was negligent, or the coverage is insufficient to accommodate a particular loss.

Check with friends and colleagues who have similar insurance needs to yours; learn from their experiences. Have they encountered settlement problems? This information will guide you in deciding which insurance company best meets your particular requirements. Personal recommendations are worth far more than glib promises of life everlasting from the insurers' friendly, caring representative looming reassuringly into your living room from a television screen!

If you have the misfortune of having to make a claim, remember to perform all the duties that are generally prescribed in the policy, or accompanying instructions. Admit nothing, apologize to no one, say or do nothing that could be interpreted as an admission of liability. Call the appropriate emergency services, if required, and while waiting for their arrival, do whatever you can to prevent further damage to life or property, provided your own safety is not put at unnecessary risk, eg, turn off the water supply in the case of a flood.

You should obtain the names and addresses of any witnesses, and make notes and drawings, or take photographs of any evidence you feel is necessary to substantiate your claim. This may be particularly useful if the damage or loss has to be repaired before the adjusters can arrive to verify a claim. A broken pane in a patio door used by small children, for instance, would obviously have to be repaired at once, in order to prevent even more serious loss through injury. The repairmen could also be contacted by the insurers if necessary.

If you have valuable possessions, such as antiques, paintings, or jewellery, make sure they are identified to the insurers, and that you have a record of any serial numbers or other characteristics, or photographs, which could confirm their loss, and help possible recovery if stolen. Antiques and pictures should be marked with your postcode and house number in an inconspicuous place, using an 'invisible' marker. This identification shows up in ultra-violet light.

Inform the insurers or broker of any loss as soon as possible, even if it is a weekend – many insurers have an emergency number. Keep the number where all members of the family will have ready access to it. When you phone to register a claim, note the date and time, and the name of the person to whom you speak. Ask the representative for specific instructions on what to do next, eg, you may be required to call your agent during office hours or to confirm in writing, and so on. Make sure you carry out instructions to the letter.

When the adjuster arrives, you will probably have to fill in a claim form, which is usually a simple task. But if you feel you need to add further information in the form of drawings, photographs, or notes, by all means do so. If the claim is straightforward and the loss is adequately covered, settlement should be reached within a few days.

On the other hand, how should you proceed if your insurers reject a claim on the grounds that the loss is not covered under the terms of your policy?

Let's assume that you live in a modest two-storey house. At the end of a long day, you like to rest your weary bones on a water bed, which you purchased new two years ago. You have obeyed its care and maintenance instructions scrupulously from the day of acquisition and, as a consequence, this wonderful invention has performed reliably.

However, you arrive home one evening to find pandemonium. Your previously unimpeachable water bed has become spontaneously and terminally incontinent; its aquatic stuffing has travelled across the bedroom floor, and has found its way to the living room below, accompanied by large chunks of plaster. Despite the frantic efforts of your spouse and two children to stem the flow of water and clean up the mess, the damage is still considerable – carpets, ceiling, walls, furniture, television, VCR – all have absorbed a generous amount of the water bed's lifeblood.

Once you have stopped the leak and completed the emergency mop-up operation to prevent any further damage, you phone the insurance broker to tell him the good news. He offers his sympathy and promises that an adjuster will phone you at your office the next morning. Having done your duty, you then drain the rest of the water from the offending bed, resurrect the original *vin ordinaire* mattress for the night, and take the family out to dinner in compensation for the unexpected adventure.

Next day, the adjuster phones your office to make an appointment to assess the damage, and appears at your home that evening as promised. You present your list of the structural, cosmetic and contents damage, and she in turn gives you a statement of claim to complete for the insurers. After a tour of the damaged site, a few more questions, the adjuster tells you she will make a report to the insurance company, and leaves with the filled-in claim form.

Two days later, you receive a phone call from your broker. He says he has been instructed to ask whether you informed the insurers that you had installed a water bed, as there is no record of it in their copy of the policy. You are of course stunned to hear such a question, and reply that as far as you are aware, you were under no obligation to notify them of such a purchase, and assumed that such a commonplace item would not require any additional insurance. The broker says he will get back to you, and you hurry home to examine your policy.

After studying the fine print for some time, you verify that the building and contents are definitely covered against water damage, whether from internal or external causes. There is no specific clause that covers damage from a water bed; indeed there is no mention of water beds anywhere in the policy nor in any of the various renewal notices and other correspondence from the insurers over the years.

Two days later, a letter arrives from the insurance company explaining that water beds are considered an additional risk, over and above normal beds, that the company requires written notification of any such furniture, and that the relevant premium will be adjusted upwards accordingly. Furthermore, since the item causing the loss was not covered, the insurer is unable to assume responsibility and settle the claim.

Dumbstruck, you phone the broker to seek his opinion, and he sadly confirms that some insurers do indeed require additional premiums for water beds. He informs you that in his opinion all you can do is pay for the damage yourself and make sure that in future your insurance covers water beds.

You now have three options: you can pursue the insurance company, the manufacturer of the water bed, or both. Your case against the insurers is fairly good, since their policy does not specifically exclude water beds. Your policy definitely covers water damage, which is what you have suffered. If insurers are wary of water beds, and require additional coverage, they, as the experts, should convey that information to their clients in writing or through a specific clause in the policy. Should the insurance company refuse to settle, the bed manufacturer should at least refund the price of the bed or provide you with a replacement (see the next chapter on tackling the retailers). Or you can refer the matter to the Insurance Ombudsman or the Personal Insurance Arbitration Service, or you can commence legal proceedings against both parties simultaneously. But since you cannot reasonably or legally expect to be paid by them both, you begin by pursuing the insurance company.

84 Fludd Street
Notarrid
WT8 0CA

Mr Des Picabell, MD
Knott Ourfawlt Insurance Ltd.
Parsimoneous Building
Welheeld
FS3 0WP

19 October 1993

Dear Mr Picabell

I hold several insurance policies, all issued by your good offices through Messrs Braak, Swerv, Skidde & Impakt Insurance Brokers Ltd, and which include Policy No 5545/HL1289 covering my house and its contents.

On 10 October 1993, my property sustained water damage through leakage from a water bed in the master bedroom. My family and I were able to stop the leak and mop up as best we could, but the damage was still sufficient to necessitate a claim under the terms of the policy mentioned above. I informed my broker that same evening, and the loss was confirmed the next day by your adjuster.

I have now received a letter from your office stating that you decline to settle my claim on the grounds that my coverage does not specify water bed indemnity. The policy in question has been in effect for more than 15 years. It was purchased because it was the most comprehensive coverage offered by your organization, and because I was under the impression that you are insurers of the highest repute – an image that is consistently emphasized in your advertising.

I have examined my policy and it is abundantly clear in section A, part 3, that the property and contents are covered against all types of water damage, from both external and internal sources. There is no mention of any item or event, let alone specific mention of water beds, that is excluded from this coverage. Therefore, by your own definition, which is quite unambiguous, I am clearly covered for the loss for which I am seeking due settlement.

I appreciate that mistakes can occur, even in a business of your long standing and reputation, and I am sure I can rely on you to resolve this matter quickly. If I do not get a satisfactory response, I will of course refer the matter to the Insurance Ombudsman.

I look forward to your immediate reply.

Yours sincerely

Kal Amity

cc Braak, Swerv, Skidde & Impakt Insurance Brokers Ltd

You have refrained from accusing the insurers of skulduggery and have merely suggested that an error must have occurred, which gives them the opportunity to save face. The gentle sting in the tail, mentioning the Insurance Ombudsman, shows that you have done your homework. In the unlikely event of further refusal to settle, then a firm response will be required, as follows:

---

84 Fludd Street
Notarrid
WT8 0CA

Mr Klauz Invallid, Chairman
Knott Ourfawlt Insurance Ltd
Parsimoneous Building
Welheeld
FS3 0WP

25 October 1993

Dear Mr Invallid

I am in receipt of a letter from your MD Mr Des Picabell, dated 23 October 1993, confirming that your company is not prepared to settle my claim of 10 October 1993, in breach of contract clearly defined in my policy number 5545/HL1289.

I trust that I can rely on your making the consequences of such ill-advised business ethics quite apparent to Mr Picabell, by letting him know that unless I receive full settlement by Tuesday, 5 November 1993, the matter will be referred to the Insurance Ombudsman.

Yours sincerely

Kal Amity

cc Braak, Swerv, Skidde & Impakt Insurance Brokers Ltd

You have given the impression that you are quite capable of pursuing the matter further and that such action is almost routine and requires no special effort on your part.

Copies of everything should be sent to your brokers, who may help in persuading the insurers to capitulate; your broker may reconsider doing business with the insurers in the future, a fact that might tip the scale in your favour.

Few companies will not readily yield under this kind of pressure, and you should soon receive a cheque in full settlement.

If this fails, when you have exhausted your attempts at receiving satisfaction from the insurers, you can take the matter to the Association of British Insurers. A reputable insurance company will be a member of the ABI and will comply with any recommendation of the ABI. But they are not obliged to do so.

If you are still dissatisfied, find out if the insurance company is a member of either the Insurance Ombudsman Bureau or the Personal Insurance Arbitration Service. Most reputable insurance companies will be a member of one or the other, though not both. In the case of the IOB scheme, you must do this within six months of receiving the decision from the insurance company. In this example, the insurance company's decision was contained in its letter dated 23 October 1993, so you must write to the IOB on, or preferably well before, 22 April 1994. The Ombudsman will look at your complaint, which you must put in writing. He will ask the insurance company to write to him with their reasons for not paying out. He will then make his decision based on this written evidence. There is no hearing and there is no fee payable for this.

The Ombudsman's decision is binding only on the insurance company, not on you. Therefore if he decides in your favour the insurance company must pay up. If he decides against you, you need not accept it, and you can then take your case to the court, as described in Chapter 10. So either way, you cannot lose out by using the Ombudsman's service.

If the insurance company is not a member of either the IOB or the PIAS, you will have to pursue your case in court straight away.

If you wish to complain about the insurance broker, you should write to the Insurance Brokers Registration Council.

Settlement following an accident

Insurance is merely a sophisticated version of gambling, with the odds stacked against the customer. When you insure your car, you are in effect betting the insurer that you are not going to have an accident within a certain period. Unfortunately, it is the insurer who determines the amount of the bet, or premium, and who keeps the stake even when you win! If you win, you might get a small discount on next year's premium. If you lose, the insurer will be anxious to keep as much of the stake as possible by settling your claim for the lowest possible price.

Insurance companies appoint adjusters, who are usually engineers or specialist motor claims assessors and they will look at a damaged vehicle and submit an 'independent' evaluation of the cost of repairs. If you disagree with the assessment, the insurance company will be quick to assure you that the firm doing the evaluation is entirely independent, completely unbiased, and not subject to any pressure or commercial loyalty. This claim is a little doubtful in practice because the assessors rely for part of their livelihood on the work they do for the insurance companies who pay their fees.

Insurance adjusters prey on the sense of guilt almost everyone involved in a car accident feels. Whether an accident is your fault or not, you will feel guilty about vehicle damage or injuries, guilty when you explain what happened to a uniformed officer in front of the mob of spectators that meets regularly at all traffic accidents, guilty when you have to confess to your insurance company or broker that you have betrayed their faith in you, and guilty when you face the mechanic who will give you an estimate. Assuming the insured will be grateful to accept any reasonable settlement, the insurer will dictate the most expedient and cheapest terms.

The purpose of insurance is to provide the funds to replace lost or damaged goods, or to restore them to the condition they were in prior to the time of loss or damage. This includes car insurance, although anyone who has made a claim must think that it is subject to a completely different set of rules. Following an motor accident, the insured will usually accept a percentage of the actual loss in compensation with only minimal protest. This is usually because it is impossible to put your car into *exactly* the same condition as before the accident.

If your rusty front wing is replaced with a new one you will end up with a better car, and the insurance company will therefore expect you to pay part of the cost. This is known as 'betterment'.

The numerous ploys the insurer practises on the unwary victim are varied and profitable. If the car is still drivable, you may be asked to take the damaged vehicle to a repair shop specified by the insurers. If the car is not drivable, it will be towed to the preferred shop.

Cooperate with the insurers, but then take your car to a repair shop of your choice for an independent estimate. If you prefer your shop to do the repairs, you should notify the insurance company of your decision, and ask for their agreement.

You may, on the other hand, decide you prefer to fix it yourself and receive a cheque for the estimated amount. But check your policy first. The terms of the policy may not allow you to do this. Invariably the insurers will tell you that they can only pay the repair shop after the job is completed.

In some cases you can do what you like with your car, no matter what terms are erroneously dictated to you. If you want to leave the car with a few dents and spend the money on a trip to France, there is absolutely nothing the insurers can do about it. Their contract with you is merely to ensure that you are reimbursed for any damage to your car, and not to supervise or enforce how the money is used after it has been paid to you.

If the estimate exceeds or is close to the present value of the vehicle, let's say £2,000, with damage costing £2,500, the insurers will tell you that they have decided to cut their losses by writing the car off. Which means that, without consulting you, they are going to scrap your car, and you are probably going to be offered a settlement as far below its real value as they can persuade you to accept. Alternatively, they might provide you with their interpretation of an equivalent vehicle.

If you are deprived of the use of your vehicle in an accident through the fault of a third party, in addition to making sure that you claim the full amount of the repair, you are entitled to the use of a hire car until the work is completed. Make certain you use one of the major hire companies even though they will be expensive; after all you wouldn't want to risk another accident by hiring an old wreck from a bargain-base ment agency! You have been rudely and blamelessly separated from your own transport, and the responsible party or their insurers must include a temporary substitute in the settlement. If you are no longer able to use your car, they are responsible for any and all costs relating to this loss. If the accident is partially or wholly your fault, or if you are making a claim on your own insurance, then you may or may not be entitled to a hire car. Check your policy.

Your policy will probably not cover all your expenses after the accident. If you are holding a third party liable for the accident, you should claim all your consequent expenses, such as any excess you had to pay, car hire costs while your car was off the road, your loss of earnings and any other expenses resulting from the accident.

If you or a passenger is physically injured, you will almost certainly wish to consult a solictor. If you do appoint a solicitor (see Chapter 10), you may still wish to settle the claim for the damaged vehicle yourself so that you can quickly effect repairs or purchase a replacement. Otherwise, ask your solicitor to make the vehicle claim separately and as soon as possible.

One fine day, you are driving home and are confronted by a red traffic signal. You obey the light but, as you sit innocently in your stationary conveyance, you hear the screech of tyres behind you, followed by the sound and feel of metal on metal. You find you and your car pushed unwillingly down the road. Luckily you are not hurt. You alight from your car to inspect the damage and make the acquaintance of your assailant.

The damage to the back of your car is extensive, but the other driver appears uninjured. You leave the cars where they are and call the police. It is particularly important not to move either vehicle, even if it means creating a massive traffic jam, for their position will be good evidence of who is liable for the incident. While you wait for the police, you exchange insurance details, names, addresses, telephone numbers, and registration numbers. The officer takes both your statements, and then, after making sure your car is still safe enough to drive, you continue on your journey. Before doing so, however, note the name, number, and station telephone number of the police officer, just in case you need to clarify any details of your claim. For the same reason, jot down the names, addresses, and telephone numbers of any witnesses.

Since you are clearly blameless in this case, you will be claiming all damages from the insurer of the vehicle that hit you. You call that company as soon as possible and make an appointment to have an adjuster verify the damage. There is no need to involve your own company or broker; you can conduct the claim yourself. However, it is a good idea to let your insurers know what has happened, making it clear that the other party is entirely liable – otherwise your accident and claim record may be blemished. Tell them you will be negotiating the settlement without their assistance.

Before you take the car to the repair shop specified by your assailant's insurers, take it to two other shops for estimates. One should be owned by a dealership specializing in selling and maintaining your make of vehicle. They will be familiar with your car, will be better able to judge any hidden damage to your make, and will probably base their estimate on new factory parts. A shop supervised by the adjuster may use secondhand parts, body filler, and 'clone' body parts made by unauthorized manufacturers. Don't forget to include the cost of a hire car and your other expenses in the estimates.

Armed with your two estimates, you arrive at the shop appointed by the adjuster. He examines the damage with the shop's estimater, and after much discussion between the two, out of earshot, he prepares his estimate.

Meanwhile, you assess the appearance of the shop. Your initial inspection does not inspire confidence. The floor is filthy and cluttered with bits of twisted metal and trim. The mechanics are wearing extremely dirty overalls. At the back of the shop, a car is being painted with no protection from the considerable dust in the shop. You are not impressed. In fact, you are concerned about the quality of the repairs – shoddy repairs will be visible to the experienced eye of a dealer and will reduce the value of your car, should you wish to sell it.

You point out your misgivings to the adjuster. He assures you that these people will do an excellent job and that he regularly recommends the shop to several different insurance companies. His estimate is £1,376.00, and the repairs will take three days.

You now present your two alternative estimates. The quote from the independent shop is £1,684.00, plus car hire for three days at £25.00 per day, for a total of £1,759.00. The dealership's repair shop quotes £1,743.00, with a four-day loan of a courtesy car for £40.00, totalling £1,783.00.

The adjuster immediately becomes defensive, and tells you that repair shops are always more realistic when dealing with adjusters than with individuals, and that since the insurance company is paying for the repairs, it has the prerogative to appoint a particular shop for the job, which in this case is the one you are visiting. Besides which, the company will not pay for a hire car because you don't use your vehicle for business. He gives you an ultimatum: if you want the job done, you will have to adhere to the insurer's terms; if you fail to comply with this 'normal' procedure, the claim will not be processed, and you will forfeit your right of settlement.

You now demonstrate that your naïvety has been somewhat overestimated. You know exactly how much you are entitled to settle for, and you have to convince him that your familiarity with the principles of car insurance is at least as good as his own. Calmly give notice that you have carefully considered the merits of the three estimates, and have decided that, without question, the dealership is best suited to make the most professional repair. To this end, you require a cheque for £1,783.00 in full settlement without delay.

If he argues that you cannot take your car to the most expensive shop, you tell him that you chose that particular quote entirely on merit and that since the damaged vehicle is owned by you, and not the insurance company, only you have the right to decide where it will be repaired.

If he protests about the hire car, point out that since the insurers are liable for all losses resulting from their client's negligence, deprivation of the use of your vehicle cannot be excluded from the claim. Furthermore, even though the car is still theoretically driveable, you are not prepared to risk another accident as a consequence of mechanical damage that may yet come to light when the vehicle is thoroughly checked during repairs. Besides which, you do not see why you should drive a damaged car when you are entitled to one in good condition. Therefore, you are going to drive to the dealership's repair shop, leave the car for repairs, and hire a suitable replacement until a cheque for the full settlement is received. All storage charges, and the accumulating cost of the hire car will be invoiced to the insurer on a weekly basis until the claim is satisfactorily settled!

Inform the adjuster that as soon as you have left your disfigured conveyance at its destination and picked up your hire car, you will be writing to his client Mr Hugh Jacksedent, MD of The Fought Knocks Insurance Company. Ask for the adjuster's business card, or if he doesn't have one, his employer's full name and address; the MD will need to know who is responsible for the circumstances that have obliged you to write to him directly.

Unless this is the first day in his chosen profession, the adjuster will be fully aware that the compensation you have specified is legitimate, and that you have the knowledge and tenacity to enforce your claim. He may authorize a settlement on your terms or he may need to get permission 'from above', which he can do by telephone from the shop.

Should you settle, ask the adjuster for the name and telephone number of the person who will be handling the settlement. You phone that person as soon as you get home to make sure that the cheque will be for the full amount and to ask when you may expect to receive it. If the amount and date for remittance meet with your approval, then you need do nothing more than wait.

If the adjuster remains unconvinced by your steadfast insistence and refuses to comply with your wishes, inform him of your intended action and then take your car and leave. When you get home, call the dealership and ask them what they charge for storage, then call a car hire agency for their daily charge, including of course all mileage and VAT.

You now write to the insurers, as follows:

---

55 Acacia Avenue
Unown City
PK1 3CV

Mr Hugh Jacksedent, MD
The Fought Knocks Insurance Company
Cardent Building
Mammon
ER2 7J

2 April 1993

Dear Mr Jacksedent

Two days ago, on 31 March, one of your clients, Mr Kit Chinsink, holder of Policy No 65983467348724 with your company, failed to observe that my car was stopped at a red traffic light and drove into the rear end of my vehicle, causing considerable damage.

After the police concluded their investigation, I exchanged the necessary personal and vehicle details with your client, and later telephoned your offices to report the collision to a Mrs Dinah Sorre. Mrs Sorre instructed me to take my car to A Salt & Vialants Car Repair, 546 Grime Street, at 1 pm today, where I would be met by your claim adjuster, Mr Don Alduk from Mak-Arber Insurance Adjusters.

On the way to the stated repair shop, I went to the trouble of obtaining two additional quotations for our mutual benefit, so that we might select the shop best suited to cope with this particular type of damage.

After Mr Alduk had inspected the car and confirmed the extent of the required repairs, I discussed the matter with him in some detail. I expressed my lack of confidence in the work I had witnessed in progress at Messrs A Salt & Vialants. We then reviewed the two quotations I had obtained earlier in the day, and upon careful analysis and reflection, I decided that the estimate (enclosed) from Grumbal-Wiyne Blunderville Ltd represented the best alternative. Their clean and efficient premises had impressed me, and the make of my car is a Blunderville, a model they specialize in.

To my astonishment, Mr Alduk greeted my decision with an alarming battery of protests, none of which were valid, including the following:

- My car had to be repaired wherever Mr Alduk dictated, irrespective of suitability or my preference.
- The claim had to be paid to the repairer on completion of the job, and not to the owner of the vehicle.
- A hire car would not be provided even though I would be deprived of my vehicle because of your client's negligence. You are legally obliged to provide compensation equal to all damages resulting from the car accident.

I can scarcely believe that a symbol of solid respectability like The Fought Knocks Insurance Company would knowingly risk its reputation by appointing a firm of adjusters so lamentably unaware of prevailing insurance legislation, and can only assume that you are unaware of the standards practised by your representatives.

Please inform me that this disgraceful performance will be investigated immediately. Meanwhile I enclose my invoice for the accident for immediate and full settlement.

Please be aware that since professional opinion is that my damaged car is too dangerous to use, I am obliged to leave the vehicle with the proposed repairers and hire a replacement until I receive a cheque in full settlement. Storage charges are £25.00 per week, and car hire is £298.54 per week. These expenses will be invoiced to you every seven days until my claim is settled.

I look forward to your early response.

Yours sincerely

Mary Dryver

Encls

The prospect of a regular weekly bill of £323.54 should elicit a quick and cooperative response.

Note that only one estimate, the one you selected, has been sent with your letter – there is no advantage to be gained by sending all three. Besides, if the MD needs further information, he can contact the adjuster or you.

You also enclose a separate invoice, so that the MD can send it down to the settlement department without delay. An invoice is resistant to adjustment and demands to be paid in total. It should include the cost of repairs, lost income, car hire and other expenses. Although you may be annoyed by the attitude and principles demonstrated by the adjuster and insurer, your claim must be kept to a reasonable and legal level. If the insurer thinks that you are out to take them for a ride, they will be very uncooperative, and your negotiating credibility will be greatly diminished. Therefore, if your car is driveable and you continue to use it, you should not invoice for storage and car hire charges.

It is unlikely that your letter and invoice will not be speedily settled, but if you have not received a cheque within about a week, a final demand is in order, as follows:

---

55 Acacia Avenue
Unown City
PK1 3CV

Mr Don Tuargu, Chairman
The Fought Knocks Insurance Company
Cardent Building
Mammon
ER2 7JW

10 April 1993

Dear Mr Tuargu

My invoice for £1,830.65 dated 2 April, sent for the attention of your MD, Mr Hugh Jacksedent, with a request for immediate settlement, appears to have escaped his attention.

I know you will be aware of your urgent legal liability concerning this matter, and trust that I may rely upon you to ensure that Mr Jacksedent remits without delay.

Failure to do so by Monday, 20 April 1993, will precipitate my isuing a summons, without further notice.

I look forward to your prompt cooperation.

Yours sincerely

Mary Dryver

cc Hugh Jacksedent, MD

Since you have not sent the chairman any details of the claim you are asking him to investigate, he will have to ascertain the urgency and content of the case by contacting Mr Jacksedent. The copy to the MD should give Mr Jacksedent further incentive to settle before embarrassing questions and investigations begin to encroach upon his usual daily routine.

In the very remote likelihood that you meet with a negative response, then a summons should be issued as soon as possible after the 20 April deadline given in your letter. But even the most obstinate insurance company will realize the futility of contesting your justifiable claim, and you should soon receive your settlement.

5

Satisfaction Guaranteed: Taking on the Retailers

Most of us must deal with retailers almost daily, buying groceries, clothing or footwear, and so on. Usually, such goods, if purchased from a reputable shop, are sound. However, occasionally merchandise may be inferior or break down prematurely.

Refusal to give a refund for faulty goods

In recent years, thanks in part to legislation, advances in communication – which speed the dissemination of bad publicity – and increased competition among manufacturers and retailers, it has become easier to obtain a refund for products that prove defective. Despite such encouraging signs of enlightenment, however, there will always be a few retailers who steadfastly refuse to take back faulty goods, even when a receipt is presented. On the other hand, customers who ask for refunds without receipts can try the patience of even the most willing and tolerant retailer; retailers can hardly be expected to remember selling merchandise to a customer six months ago, or refund money for merchandise that may have been purchased from another supplier.

Having said that, I am reminded of a friend's recent experience: her television cable converter died after two years of reliable service. The item was purchased with a one-year guarantee from a large chain of retailers, which will remain anonymous. My friend took the deceased converter to the nearest outlet, without a receipt, and offered it to the assistant. The assistant gave it hardly a glance, and said, 'These often seem to come back,' and promptly gave my friend a brand-new converter – a newer and better model than the original. So there is hope!

All goods that are sold by a shop to a private customer must be in accordance with their description, fit for their purpose and be of merchantable quality. If goods are faulty, you will be entitled either to your money back or to compensation for loss caused by the goods being faulty. You can only get your money back if you have not accepted the goods. You will have accepted the goods if you have treated the goods as your own, attempted a repair, expressed satisfaction with them, or simply kept them for even quite a short time.

If you are entitled to your money back you need not accept an exchange or a credit note. If, however, you are only entitled to compensation, you may be more willing to accept an exchange, a credit note or a free repair.

There are steps you can take to reduce the likelihood of your purchases failing prematurely: use the goods only for their intended purpose (for instance a cellular telephone may deteriorate rapidly if it's used while scuba-diving!); pay attention to special instructions or requirements. If you keep your receipts, use your purchases for the purpose intended, and do not treat them to any unrealistic excesses, you will have done all that is required to substantiate a claim if the goods fail to perform adequately or for as long as could reasonably be anticipated.

Let us assume that you purchased an expensive pair of high-heeled shoes to wear to the office. Since they were rather more than you could afford at the time, you look after them with more care than normal and only wear them in clement weather. One fine day ten weeks later, the local bus drivers are working to rule (which rule, and what dark secret it harbours, nobody knows), and thus you decide to walk to work, wearing The Shoes. As you step off the pavement at a junction, there is a sharp noise from your right heel as it parts company with the rest of the shoe, and you feel yourself falling. Fortunately your descent is arrested by a fellow pedestrian. You hobble over to a nearby while-you-wait heel-and-sole shop, where the shoemaker informs you that the shoes are so poorly made, he won't fix them! You have no choice but to proceed to the office barefoot.

After work, you pay a visit to the department store that sold you the footwear. You ask for the manager, who is in and willingly grants an audience. However, the manager's accommodating and obsequious manner swiftly deteriorates as, while examining the invalid shoes, she conducts an intensive interrogation about their use. You calmly answer all her questions and inform her that you have the receipt at home and can produce it the next day, if necessary. The manager informs you that since they are fashion shoes and not walking shoes, they have been subjected to far greater strain than they were designed to withstand, and that she can see nothing at all wrong with the workmanship. In fact, the shoes are from a very reputable manufacturer, and this is the first time anyone has returned with a complaint. She refuses to accept liability even with the receipt. Aghast at such callous dismissal, you protest no further, and retreat complete with damaged shoes.

It is probably not practical for most footwear manufacturers to offer a guarantee for a specific length of time since some people go through shoes almost as quickly as most people use paper handkerchiefs. Having bought one pair of shoes, such people could conceivably have free replacements at the expense of the manufacturer for the rest of their lives! However, it is reasonable to expect a reputable retailer or manufacturer to judge individual complaints according to their merit.

Now it is time to address the matter in writing. Write to the Head Office of the retailer since they are responsible for selling you the shoes and offered no written or verbal warning that their life expectancy was two and a half months. Your contract is with the retailer, not with the manufacturer. By all means, though, send a copy of the correspondence to the manufacturer.

The letter to the Head Office could read as follows:

Flat 40
92 Tipe Avenue
Shuless
HD5 3VT

Mr Howie Kondme, MD
Pathrew Thenoez Stores Ltd
100 Sezermy Street
Kutthrote
KF9 5PA

25 October 1993

Dear Mr Kondme

On 21 August 1993, I purchased from your shop in the High Street, Shuless, a pair of Bunyan Akes shoes, for the price of £97.99 (photocopy of receipt enclosed).

I particularly chose Bunyan Akes, as they have a good reputation and their advertising always strongly suggests that their products are well made and comfortable. I elected to make my investment at one of your shops, since I have been a customer for many years, you always have a good selection of merchandise, and I always receive quick and courteous service.

I was thoroughly distressed, therefore, when, while I was strolling to work, a heel snapped right off one of my new shoes as I was crossing a busy junction. Although shaken, I was fortunately not injured, and took the shoes to a nearby shoe repairer to see what could be done. The shoemaker refused to repair the shoes because they were of such poor quality!

I took the shoes back to your shop that evening, where I was told by your footwear department manager, Ms Anne Olbute, that the break was caused by excessive walking! I am sure that you will agree that Ms Olbute's analysis is, to say the least, less than accurate; I have rarely worn the shoes in the short time since buying them, as can be verified by the lack of wear on the soles and heels, and have never worn them in the rain or snow.

There must, therefore, be a fault in the design or manufacturing process of which I am an innocent victim. Clearly, the shoes were not of merchantable quality, and I will be most grateful to receive your authorization of a complete refund of the purchase price.

No doubt you will require the shoes so that you can send them back to Bunyan Akes, and I will be pleased to leave them at your shop when I collect my refund.

I would appreciate your settling this matter at your earliest convenience.

Yours sincerely

Tanya Hyde

cc U C Clogg, MD, Bunyan Akes Footwear Ltd

In your letter you have stressed that you are a regular and normally appreciative customer, that possible physical injury was narrowly avoided, and that the goods do not live up to the standards claimed in advertisements. You have refrained from suggesting any deliberate malpractice by the shop. At the same time, you are concerned by the department manager's reaction, which must be redressed if the shop is to retain a loyal customer.

If the shop refuses to comply with your wishes, then another letter should be sent as follows:

Mr Howie Kondme, MD
Pathrew Thenoez Stores Ltd
100 Sezermy Street
Kutthrote
KF9 5PA

29 October 1993

Dear Mr. Kondme,

I have read your letter of 28 October and I am astonished to learn that you are not prepared to authorize the refund to which I am clearly entitled.

I find it difficult to believe that an organization the size of Pathrew Thenoez Stores does not employ anyone with sufficient technical knowledge to recognize a sincere and valid claim initiated by the poor workmanship in goods sold.

Unless the amount claimed, £97.99, is settled in full by Tuesday, 12 November 1993, a court summons will be issued without further notice. The damaged shoes will be produced as evidence at the trial.

Yours sincerely

Tanya Hyde

cc U C Clogg, MD, Bunyan Akes Footwear Ltd
Wun Hung Lo, Trading Standards Dept, Shuless Council

There may be various retail associations you can contact, such as the Footwear Distributors Federation which publishes a code of practice for its members. Your local library, Citizens' Advice Bureau or other advice agency or the Office of Fair Trading should be able to track them down.

When you send copies to these agencies, include all previous correspondence so that they will have all the facts. The more associations the merrier; the shop probably wouldn't want its reputation brought to their attention. This second and final letter, with its copies going to appropriate regulatory bodies, should certainly encourage the shop to suddenly see your point of view in a more accommodating light, and a refund should be on its way with little delay. Otherwise you will have to proceed to the small claims court.

Merchandise breaks down after warranty expires

Have you ever wondered why some goods seem to have an internal clock that starts ticking as soon as you make your purchase, and then expires immediately after the guarantee has done likewise? How often your purchase is used makes no difference. The guarantee runs out on Tuesday, and the item dies in sympathy on Wednesday.

Returning the goods to the vendor and pleading that the warranty be honoured as it is only a day or two on the wrong side of the expiry date usually proves to be an exercise in futility. You will invariably be told that if the manufacturer had intended to supply a guarantee of 366 days, this would have been printed on the warranty. Therefore, at one second after midnight following the day of expiry, you are entirely responsible for the expense of repairing or replacing the faulty goods.

With few exceptions, most customers will assume their rights are indeed limited to the conditions imposed by the manufacturer or retailer, and after a brief attempt to obtain a sympathetic extension, they give up. This is good news for the manufacturers; they save a great deal of money by not having to replace faulty goods, and their profits soar when customers have to purchase a replacement. Unscrupulous manufacturers even reduce the quality of their goods to last only as long as the warranty. Such manufacturers may risk losing customers to competitors, but the overall increase in business usually outweighs any losses.

Most warranties cover the minimum period that manufacturers can comfortably get away with, and may include all manner of escape clauses, such as excluding labour, shipping costs to the factory for repair, damage to user or property as a consequence of failure of the goods, and so forth. But if a long warranty is unreasonable to a manufacturer, a short one is unfair to the customer.

Any warranty or guarantee that a manufacturer or retailer offers you will be in addition to your rights under consumer protection legislation. Indeed, it is a criminal offence for a retailer to suggest that you have fewer rights than the law gives you. Whatever the guarantee may say, the goods must still be of merchantable quality, fit for their purpose and be in accordance with their description.

Let's suppose you recently bought a vacuum cleaner, which has broken down after 12 months and one day. You take it back to the shop where it was purchased, and you are told that the motor has burned out. The bad news is that the warranty expired at the end of 12 months, so you will have to pay for the repair. The good news is that the new motor will come with a three-month warranty!

You protest that you have used the machine carefully, but to no avail, and you elect to leave with the machine unrepaired. When you get home, you call two alternative repairers, describe the problem, and ask them if a burned-out motor is a typical fault of this particular model. You are told that it is, and that you can expect the new one not to last more than a few months. In addition, the two repair shops confirm that three years would be a reasonable life expectancy for a vacuum cleaner like yours.

You now call the manufacturer of your recalcitrant machine, and ask for the service manager. Make sure you get his name before you speak to him. You will be making notes of the conversation, which may be used as evidence against the company later on. You tell him that you would like his expert opinion on a machine, made by his firm, that you are considering purchasing. Explain that your principal concern is reliability, and his opinion will be of great assistance in helping you decide whether the model in question is suited to your requirements.

You are pleased to be inundated with glowing testimony about the unparalleled performance and reliability of the marvellous machine, while your own defunct example sits forlornly on the floor. He assures you that it should be entirely problem-free for a good five years and that he personally knows of several that have been running like clockwork for much longer. You thank him kindly for his valuable and generous advice, and assure him that his firm will now enjoy the benefit of your immediate attention thanks in no small part to his very persuasive convictions!

A letter to the manufacturer is in order, as follows:

---

22 Spotlis Avenue
Sweaping Mounds
GH6 8CT

Mr Neal Toscrubb, MD
Oarful Appliances Ltd
Gleaming Towers
Nophilthe
YS7 3PQ

29 October 1993

Dear Mr Toscrubb

I am the owner of a Muk Maniak vacuum cleaner, purchased from your shop at 274 Fuzebloane Street, Sweaping Mounds.

This is an excellent machine in all respects, and I really appreciate its light weight, powerful suction, and unusually quiet operation, which allows me to hear the telephone or doorbell while I am vacuuming.

Unfortunately, during routine use two days ago, my Muk Maniak abruptly stopped, for no apparent reason, and I took it back to the shop. The machine was examined by the manager, Mr Nofix, who informed me the motor had burned out and would have to be replaced.

I expressed surprise at this diagnosis since it was the much advertised reputation for trouble-free operation that convinced me to replace my old vacuum with a Muk Maniak. I received a further shock when Mr Nofix refused to repair my machine, even though it is only just over 12 months old. Apparently the guarantee is valid for only 12 months, and he is not able to authorize repairs past that time, even when the defect has occurred through no fault of the user.

I checked the model's service reputation with a number of other repair shops, and I was most interested to learn that the motors on this model are prone to burning out prematurely and that even the replacements are subject to the same fate! Yet, curiously enough, when I called the manufacturer to seek the opinion of their service manager, Mr Li Ing, he expressed his enthusiasm and confidence in the Muk Maniak, and assured me that it 'should be entirely problem-free for a good five years' and that he knows of many that have lasted for considerably longer.

Confusing, isn't it?

I am sure you will agree that a well-built vacuum cleaner merits a warranty that accurately reflects the confidence the makers have in its workmanship, and I cannot believe that your company expects the model in question to start giving trouble after only 12 months. It is clear to me that the particular model that you sold to me was not of merchantable quality.

I look forward to your confirmation that my vacuum cleaner will be repaired free of charge at once, with no cost to me.

Yours sincerely

Bess Tufikxit

cc U R Nofix, Manager, Oarful Appliances, Sweaping Mounds

The message should be abundantly clear. You have done your homework and discovered that Muk Maniak machines are dropping like flies throughout the land while the manufacturer's service manager continues to sing their praises with no concern for reality. Mr Toscrubb should anticipate the possible adverse publicity if he does not act quickly to placate you. But, alas, he is not swayed by your flattery and diligence, and refuses to provide you with a repair. You now write him another helpful letter, as follows:

---

22 Spotlis Avenue
Sweaping Mounds
GH6 8CT

Mr Neal Toscrubb, MD
Oarful Appliances Ltd
Gleaming Towers
Nophilthe
YS7 3PQ

6 November 1993

Dear Mr Toscrubb

I was very surprised to receive your letter of 4 November, which fails adequately to address my problem with a vacuum cleaner purchased from your shop in Sweaping Mounds.

I find it extraordinary to learn that a large company with a reputation for quality and fair trading like yours is now selling goods that are not of merchantable quality. Furthermore, you refuse to repair breakdowns that occur as a result of these inadequacies.

Unless I receive written authorization for my machine to be repaired free of charge, by 13 November 1993, I will have the cleaner repaired and invoice you for the full amount, plus my incurred expenses. Should your company not settle the invoice, I will not hesitate to issue a court summons.

Yours sincerely

Bess Tufikxit

cc U R Nofix, Manager, Oarful Appliances, Sweaping Mounds

In the unlikely event that your wishes are still not being taken seriously, have the cleaner repaired, and send your invoice to the retailer, as promised. There is no need to include another letter with it.

Bess Tufikxit
22 Spotlis Avenue
Sweaping Mounds
GH6 8CT

Oarful Appliances Ltd
Gleaming Towers
Nophilthe
YS7 3PQ

18 November 1993

For the attention of Neal Toscrubb, MD

INVOICE

For replacement of prematurely failed motor to Muk Maniak vacuum cleaner, supplied by Oarful Appliances	£137.58
Expenses (visits to repair shop, postage, etc)	£105.00
Total	£242.58

Terms: Payment by return. Overdue accounts attract interest at 1.5% per month.

UNLESS THIS ACCOUNT IS SETTLED IN FULL BY MONDAY 2 DECEMBER 1993, A COURT SUMMONS WILL BE ISSUED WITHOUT FURTHER NOTICE.

An invoice demands attention, and your persistence will show that you are unstoppable, which should produce a cheque.

The expenses may or may not be included, but if they are not, then further attempts to collect them are probably inadvisable.

6

Battles on the Home Front: Repairs and Renovations

A home, no matter how sweet, will need repairs from time to time. It would be prudent to keep a list of reliable tradesmen – electrician, roofer, appliance repairer, and plumber – close to your phone as you would other emergency numbers.

Deficient home renovation

Building an addition or remodelling a home can involve considerable expense and inconvenience. Most homeowners are at the mercy of suppliers, contractors, designers and architects, and can find their tempers sorely tried by the mess, disruption and constant presence of strangers in their home.

Something can go wrong at any stage, delaying completion and adding further to the expense, even with a good contractor at the helm. Clearly, prevention is better than cure. To this end, selecting a good architect or designer and a competent and honest contractor is essential. A recommendation from a trustworthy friend, neighbour, or professional organization is the best way to find both a contractor and an architect.

Meet several architects, and discuss what you want built. You should have a budget in mind, and be clear about how architects establish their fees and how much the necessary drawings for your job will cost. Ask to see pictures of past projects, and check references. The architect you choose will prepare conceptual drawings from which you will select a design. After approving the final drawings, ask your architect to obtain quotes from at least three contractors. This will give you an opportunity to meet the three bidders and discuss the project with them.

If you are proceeding without an architect, you should also get quotes from three contractors. Invite them to the site. Beware of contractors who arrive at a price too quickly, particularly if the job is large or complex. A contractor who can start work immediately could also be doubtful: his ready availability may mean there is little demand for his type of workmanship. And beware of contractors who want a large deposit – they could be fly-by-night operators.

When assessing quotes, don't necessarily accept the lowest, particularly if it is way below the next competitor's quote. The bidder may be using poor materials and unsuitable short cuts, may have missed an important detail of the specification, or he may be deliberately bidding low to secure the project and will bill you for the 'extras' later.

Once you have selected a contractor and obtained planning permission from your local authority, you will want to discuss any possible problems, starting and completion dates, and a payment schedule before signing the contracts. As a general rule, the payments should always favour you, the customer. Apart from any legal entitlement to hold back on each payment made, you should not pay more than about two-thirds of the percentage of work completed. You will then always be comfortably in credit in the event the builder or one of his subcontractors defaults. Make sure you have a fixed price contract: a cost-plus arrangement might continue to cost and plus for much longer than you bargained for! Read *How to Geet Work Done on Your Home* by R D Buchanan (Kogan Page).

When you begin building, be prepared for some disruption and inconvenience. Your contractor is your colleague; if you have complaints, discuss them with him calmly and away from his employees and subcontractors. If you are pleased with the work, draw his attention to it, preferably within earshot of the employees who actually did it! A few well-placed, sincere compliments will go far to soften hostilities should a dispute arise.

Should you have any new ideas or changes, you should discuss them with the contractor, not the subtrader involved. It is the contractor who is responsible for supervising all the trades on the job, and he has to know exactly what they are doing to maintain efficient coordination. Asking the heating contractor to move a duct over may seem a minor request, but it may be difficult for the plumber to route his pipes around it.

By all means offer the crew refreshments from time to time. But under no circumstances offer beer or any alcoholic beverages; your liability could be brought into question in the event of a subsequent injury or damage to property, no matter how little alcohol was actually offered or consumed. And while good relations with those who are working on the job is no bad thing, don't spend so much time talking to employees that you distract them from their work. Most are paid on an hourly basis, and your contractor will be keen to see that his pounds are spent on productivity, not conversational dexterity.

Be prepared for unanticipated problems, and make sure you know the difference between an extra and work that should have been anticipated in the estimates. If framing behind a wall is found to be rotten, then replacing it is clearly an unanticipated, or extra, expense. On the other hand, plaster repairs to a wall after new plumbing is installed are predictable and should have been included in the original price. Make sure any alterations to the contract or extras are agreed to in writing, including the exact cost, no matter how small. Extras can add up, and unless they are kept strictly on record, the increased costs can be surprisingly high.

A contractor can be affected by events beyond his control – strikes, material shortages, and so on. Expect everything to take longer than anticipated, and plan accordingly. And if you spot something that is below standard or that has not been carried out according to the plans, bring it to the contractor's attention at once. The longer you delay, the more difficult and expensive it will become to make corrections. For example, it is easy to move a bathroom vanitory unit before the fixtures are installed, but difficult and time-consuming once the tiles and fixtures are in.

Despite all precautions, however, disputes do occur. Should you become involved in a disagreement with your contractor, try to compromise. If you cannot arrive at an acceptable compromise by yourselves, agree to binding arbitration by your architect, if you have one, or another knowledgeable consultant. It is important to find a quick and amicable solution, so that work can proceed without undue interruption.

Let us assume that you have just survived a major kitchen renovation, which was finished several days ago, and you have now spotted some irritating and potentially expensive deficiencies: one of the counter tops has some chips and scratches that were touched up with paint, which has now worn off; some of the new ceramic tiles have come loose; and the subfloor squeaks. If you are using an architect or other qualified independent adviser, seek their opinion as to the validity of your complaint.

You phone the contractor to ascertain his willingness to correct the problems, and after several failed attempts to locate him, and no effort on his part to return your calls, you are obliged to put your grievances in writing, as follows:

---

78 Daybree Crescent
Hacienda
DS6 4JK

Mr Lee Kinapype, MD
Deral Liction Construction Ltd
211 Ivasive Lane
Hacienda
DS9 3XL

1 March 1993

Dear Lee

You will be pleased to learn that I am very happy with our new kitchen.

Before you present your final account for payment, however, I should be most grateful if you could drop by to give me your valuable opinion on a couple of defects that appear to be in need of correction: the counter top on the north wall has some chips and scratches, and some of the tiles by the back entrance door have come loose, possibly because the floor in that area creaks slightly. I am sure the occasional flaw can occur in any major renovation, but we would not like your otherwise excellent workmanship to be marred by uncorrected problems.

I did phone you a few times last week to let you know what had happened, but I daresay you have been very busy and unable to return my calls. Please phone me as soon as possible to let me know when it will be convenient for you to inspect the counter top and ceramic floor.

I look forward to hearing from you.

Yours sincerely

Luke Athemess

Since you were on first-name terms with the contractor, there is no reason why you should not continue to be so. You are trying to be as pleasant as possible in order to persuade him to bring the job up to his high standards, as well as your own, and the first communication should be phrased in suitably amicable expectation.

If you do not hear from him within three days, you may phone to enquire if your letter has been received. If there is still no response, a further letter should be sent, as follows:

---

78 Daybree Crescent
Hacienda
DS6 4JK

Mr Lee Kinapype, MD
Deral Liction Construction Ltd
211 Ivasive Lane
Hacienda
DS9 3XL

7 March 1993

Dear Lee

Further to my earlier telephone calls, letter of 1 March and message left two days ago, your immediate response is now urgently requested.

Aside from the cosmetic and structural concerns that I have outlined, I am worried that the loose tiles could result in personal injuries, particularly to young children playing in the kitchen. The consequences of an accident do not bear thinking about, and I know you will share my anxiety that all preventive measures be taken without delay.

Kindly respond at the earliest opportunity.

Yours sincerely

Luke Athemess

Deliver the letter by hand, if convenient, and post a copy as well. This will ensure that he receives it, and will emphasize the degree of urgency and insistence that you are trying to convey. The prospect of a legal action for personal injury will serve as a powerful incentive to respond, and the unmistakable tone of your correspondence, together with his awareness that the final bill has yet to be settled, should produce a quick result.

And it does. The next day Mr Kinapype phones to say he will be over later that evening to take a look at the alleged deficiencies. He arrives as promised, but he protests liability for the counter top on the grounds that it has now been used for two weeks; he implies that the scratches and chips have been inflicted through domestic carelessness. Furthermore, he refuses to accept responsibility for the loose tiles; he accuses the occupants of the house of subjecting them to heavy traffic and abuse while they were still in the process of setting. You point out the paint touch-ups in the scratched countertop, but an explanation is not forthcoming, and he insists it was in perfect shape when installed, and was still so on completion of the job.

You assure him that no one went near the new tiles for three days after they were installed, and you demonstrate that the subfloor creaks; but he continues to insist that a minor creak would have no effect on the adherence of the tiles, and that they must have been subject to some abuse.

The discussion leads nowhere, and you are told that nothing can be done until the bill, which he has with him and presents to you, has been paid. As soon as the account is settled, he adds, any repairs can be made, but he is not liable for them, and they will have to be paid for just like any other job. Naturally, you do not pay the balance owing on his invoice, but without allowing the discussion to develop into an unpleasant argument, you invite him to leave, and let him know he will be hearing from you very shortly. Fortunately, the amount you still owe him is considerably more than the repairs would cost, but you still have to arrange for the work to be done, and if possible, conclude matters without too much trouble or delay.

It will be in your interest to prevent your relationship with the contractor from becoming irrevocably hostile – you may need to call him back in the future. Another letter is therefore in order.

---

78 Daybree Crescent
Hacienda
DS6 4JK

Mr Lee Kinapype, MD
Deral Liction Construction Ltd
211 Ivasive Lane
Hacienda
DS9 3XL

9 March 1992

Dear Lee

Further to our meeting last night, I am sorry that we could not arrive at a mutually agreeable solution to the counter top and tile problems discussed. You have my absolute assurance that none of my family damaged the counter top in question; the obvious paint touch-ups leave little doubt that the responsibility is not ours.

As for the loose tiles, I made quite sure that the floor was not walked upon or used in any way for three days after the tiles were installed. The tiles have loosened in an area that is not subject to heavy usage; therefore had we used the floor prematurely there would have been additional loose tiles where traffic is much heavier. It seems very likely, therefore, that the creaking subfloor is indeed the cause of the disturbance – an inflexible tile will not adhere properly to a flexible floor.

I realize that having to come back to remedy these problems is an annoyance, particularly since your suppliers or subcontractors are presumably responsible for the defects. However, I have great respect for your workmanship and integrity, and your cooperation in ensuring that the necessary repairs are completed without delay will be greatly appreciated.

The alternative, which is for me to hire another contractor to do the work, is not an option I would willingly choose, as I am anxious to settle the balance of your invoice in full. I am unable to do so until the matter is resolved, preferably by your company, and I know you would not want to incur the expense of a competitor having to come and complete your otherwise excellent renovation.

Please let me know that you will be able to do the required work without delay.

Yours sincerely

Luke Athemess

This should bring the desired response. In the unlikely event that he still refuses to cooperate, then you will have to obtain a couple of alternative quotes for the repairs, and send a final opportunity for him to comply with his obligations, as follows:

---

78 Daybree Crescent
Hacienda
DS6 4JK

Mr Lee Kinapype, MD
Deral Liction Construction Ltd
211 Ivasive Lane
Hacienda
DS9 3XL

12 March 1993

Dear Lee

I am sorry that you still feel unable to complete the necessary repairs to my kitchen, as described in my previous letters of 1, 7 and 9 March.

I have consequently had to seek an alternative contractor to finish the job satisfactorily, and the firm I have selected will do the work for the inclusive price of £643.00, which I shall be obliged to deduct from my cheque in settlement of your final account.

I still much prefer that you do the work but, unless you let me know by 16 March that you are willing to do so, I shall reluctantly proceed with the alternative quotation.

I trust that I may hear from you before 16 March.

Yours sincerely

Luke Athemess

If he does not comply with your last demand, have the work done by someone else, and deduct the amount from the final payment. That should conclude the matter. Most contractors will respond before their work is given to a rival, so protracted correspondence is not usually necessary. If you had been using an architect, you would, of course, have asked him or her to intervene on your behalf.

Overcharge by plumber

Practically everyone has a horror story to tell about their experiences with a plumber. Ah, the much maligned plumber, struggling to earn an honest living in insanitary conditions, often called out at unsocial hours, and yet he is seen as unpunctual, untidy, unreliable, and enormously wealthy through charging prices that might have made Al Capone consider a change of career!

Some plumbers are more reliable than others, just as some are more expensive than others. Inevitably, there are those who take advantage of a customer's predicament, especially when the job has to be done immediately. When you are presented with the bill, which will probably be more than you expected, how do you know whether you are being overcharged?

To alleviate any surprises, you should ask for an estimate first. A plumber may be reluctant to commit himself, but if his estimate is too high, and he refuses to negotiate, you have the option of sending him on his way and hiring another plumber. Of course, you risk a further delay and the next estimate might turn out to be even higher than the one you already have, and by the time you call the original plumber again, he may be out on another job and unable, or unwilling, to fit you into his new schedule.

If you get an estimate, the plumber can charge you more, but not an unreasonable amount more. If you get a quotation, he must stick to this price whatever happens. If no price is agreed, he can only charge you a 'reasonable' amount. Phone other plumbers and ask how much they charge; this will give you a good idea of what a 'reasonable' amount is.

Let's assume that one wet and windy night, you are woken by incessant barking from your dog. You plod angrily downstairs to offer advice to the unfaithful canine, who is sitting at the top of the basement stairs, but you are distracted by an unsavoury odour. Vigorously brushing Fido aside, you switch on the basement lights to discover that the subterranean portion of your house is now several inches deep in a liquid that is definitely not pure rainwater! The source of the infiltration appears to be a floor drain, which would indicate a blockage somewhere outside the house.

After a frenzied search in the Yellow Pages, you call a 24-hour emergency service plumber that guarantees service within the hour. Sure enough, about 55 minutes after your call, two men arrive with various large items of equipment. They work in the rising waters for about three hours, and finally a shout of triumph precedes the welcome sight of water going down the drain. The plumbers inform you that the blockage was caused by debris that had collected in the pipe where it had been cracked by a tree root.

As they pack up their tools, you tremble with anticipation; you can hardly wait to see the bill. To your absolute horror, the invoice is even worse than expected – £980.00. You ask for a breakdown of the amount and are told that this is the standard charge for the job, and it includes a surcharge for working during the night and at short notice. The plumber is not keen to offer details of his hourly rate; he insists that this is not an excessive price for emergency work, and that no one has ever questioned it before. Besides, he does not set the rates, he just does the work, and is not allowed to leave the job site until it is paid.

So, how should you proceed? Fortunately, there are several factors in your favour, the most important being that you have achieved your objective, which was to have the blockage cleared quickly. Whatever happens, the probability of the blockage being reinstalled is reasonably remote! And payment is still in your hands, which is a definite advantage. It will be very difficult for the plumber to extract payment from you if the size of the bill cannot be satisfactorily explained, especially if you are willing to pay an amount you consider reasonable. (Partial payment demonstrates that you are willing to settle, provided the amount is reasonable, and also leaves a reduced amount outstanding, which may not be worth collecting. If you paid the full amount and tried to recover part of it later, you would probably have to resort to the courts.)

If the plumbers refuse to leave until they are paid, then you must inform them that they no longer have your permission to be on the premises, and therefore they are trespassing. If they insist on remaining against your instructions, warn them that you are going to call the police, particularly if they behave in a threatening manner. (If you must follow through, remember that disagreements over payment will be of no interest to the police because they are strictly a civil matter. So, when calling, refrain from describing the commercial aspect of the transaction. The police are only interested in upholding the law, and ensuring your personal safety.)

To encourage the plumbers to leave willingly, you tell them you have every intention of paying the bill, but not before it has been thoroughly analyzed by their boss – the proprietor or MD. Get his full name, title and telephone number, and what time he will be in his office. Ask the plumbers for their names and numbers as well. This will show them that you are serious about seeking a reduction and that you are not just looking for an excuse not to pay them. Eventually your strategy works, and they depart.

First thing in the morning, you phone the proprietor to explain the situation and confirm your willingness to negotiate a fair price. If you write without phoning first, the attending plumbers will have reported your non-payment before your letter arrives, and the proprietor, not having heard from you, may assume an aggressive and fixed viewpoint, which will make your negotiations more difficult. Before you phone, check with two or three alternative plumbers from the Yellow Pages, to see what they would have charged for the same job. If they are reluctant to say, you could mention that this has happened before and that you seem to recall it costing about £325.00 – or some other figure well below the amount of the invoice in dispute. This will precipitate a reaction, and will make it easy for them to give you a more accurate estimate. Once you have three estimates, make your phone call to the company that has just done the job.

You begin by complimenting the proprietor on his men's speedy response to your emergency and the short time it took them to locate and clear the blockage. This underlines the limited time the job took, reduces the justification for a large bill, and flatters his operation! Then, you inform him that you regret that you could not pay the bill in full as you are sure a mistake has occurred. You give him the three alternative quotes and stress that they are all for less than half the amount he has charged! You tell him you do not want to waste his valuable time in haggling, and are more than willing to pay him the amount of the highest of the three.

However, he becomes abusive, and you cut the conversation short, telling him you will let him know your intentions in writing.

---

56 Ouze Avenue
Poulinseler
YS3 4RT

Mr Gord Elpus, MD
Brane Drain Ltd
88 Block Street
Poulinseler
YS2 2QT

5 November 1991

Dear Mr Elpus

Further to our telephone conversation this morning concerning the blockage that was cleared by your workers earlier today, I confirm that I was pleased with the speed at which they turned out at short notice, and that the drain now seems to be working as it should.

Your invoice No 3268, for the sum of £980.00 for the work, however, appears to have been computed erroneously since the job was completed in just over three hours. I discussed this alarming amount with your Mr Sludje, who was in charge of the operation, but he was unable to help because the accounts are not under his control. I am therefore obliged to return the invoice for your attention, so that it can be corrected to a more realistic figure.

As a matter of interest, I checked with three of your competitors to see what they would have charged for the same job, and the quotes I was offered varied from £385.00 to £440.00. These prices are for their emergency service, and include VAT. Since you provided excellent service, which I would be pleased to recommend to anyone who may be unfortunate enough to suffer a similar emergency, I would be perfectly happy to settle your account at the highest of the three alternative quotes.

As soon as I am in receipt of your satisfactorily revised account, I will make full settlement by return post.

Yours sincerely

Ali Gayter

Encl

No suggestion of extortion has been made. You are careful to avoid putting the company on the defensive, so that it will be easy for Mr Elpus to explain away the overcharge as an accounting error.

You return the invoice with the letter; since you have no intention of paying it, there is no need to keep it. The ball is back in the company's court. But Mr Elpus is unwilling to match the prices of his competitors, and returns his invoice with a demand for payment in full. You reply as follows:

---

56 Ouze Avenue
Poulinseler
YS3 4RT

Mr Gord Elpus, MD
Brane Drain Ltd
88 Block Street
Poulinseler
YS6 2QT

12 November 1992

Dear Mr Elpus

I have received your letter dated 10 November and the returned invoice No 3268.

I find it completely unacceptable that you persist in charging me £980.00 for a total of seven man-hours' work! This is more than double the amount charged by the most expensive of your competitors, as I explained in my letter of 5 November. I am perfectly willing to pay you a fair price for the job, and my offer to settle this matter by agreeing to match the most expensive figure quoted by your competitors is still valid. Anything in excess of this amount is out of the question. I therefore enclose a cheque for the sum of £440.00 in full and final settlement of your account.

Kindly issue a receipt by return of post.

Yours sincerely

Ali Gayter

Encl

Your letter is firm and clear, and should convince him that this is absolutely all you are going to pay. Enclosing payment before the dispute has been settled is a calculated risk, with the odds in your favour. You have paid him at least the amount to which he is entitled, possibly more if the quote on which you based your payment is expensive. So you can be quite sure that the job was still very profitable, and that the proprietor does not have outstanding expenses from the work not covered by your cheque.

Had you decided not to pay anything at all, he would be justified in seeking redress through the courts. But you have established the prevailing rates, and paid accordingly, and he will realize that it will be difficult to get a favourable decision from a court.

If there is further correspondence with the opposition, do not leave any communication unanswered. A short reply to any further demands for payment could read as follows:

---

56 Ouze Avenue
Poulinseler
YS3 4RT

Mr Gord Elpus, MD
Brane Drain Ltd
88 Block Street
Poulinseler
YS2 2QT

17 November 1992

Dear Mr Elpus

I am in receipt of your letter dated 16 November.

I regret that you do not appear to understand that the sum of £438.00, which I remitted on 12 November, is in full and final settlement of your account dated 5 November.

Demands for further monies are completely unjustified, and will not be met.

If you feel that the prospect of your using alternative methods to pursue the matter will alter my position, I am afraid you are very much mistaken.

Yours sincerely

Ali Gayter

This letter is brief and makes your position clear. You will notice that the letter does not address any points that may have been raised by Mr Elpus. You are past the stage of discussion, and only wish to convey that you are tired of his time wasting and futile persistence.

He may retain lawyers who send you a letter threatening action within a specified time. Such a letter is unlikely to result in the litigation threatened or implied, but will require a reply to call their bluff. Something like this usually works quite well:

---

56 Ouze Avenue
Poulinseler
YS3 4RT

Thrett, Snarll & Pounts, Solicitors
Charck Lane
Poulinseler
YS3 2HX

28 November 1992

Dear Sirs

I received a letter dated 24 November from your Ms Barb E D Thrett, purportedly acting on behalf of Brane Drain Ltd.

If Ms Thrett wishes me to elaborate on any points that she may find confusing, I would be pleased to do so before a judge, at her earliest convenience.

Yours sincerely

Ali Gayter

cc Gord Elpus, Brane Drain Ltd

No ambiguity in this one! Lawyers' letters don't scare me. If you want to sue, then go ahead.

You have deliberately departed from the practice of addressing mail to the principal. This shows that, although Ms Thrett is clearly a senior partner in the firm, you are not impressed by either her credentials or her letter, and that by not addressing her directly you are not taking her very seriously. Your complete lack of concern will raise doubts as to the merit of pursuing the matter any further.

7

Presumed Innocent: Taking on the Lawyers

Most of us have developed an unhealthy dose of awe for the professionals and a high tolerance for unprofessional behaviour and business practices. A well-worded letter will be highly effective when dealing with solicitors, unaccustomed as they are to receiving correspondence from mere mortals.

Your solicitor overcharges you

It is hoped that your skills in communication will help to resolve most of the injustices life sends your way. Inevitably, though, nearly everyone will need to consult a lawyer about some matter at some time. Not necessarily for the advice or collection of a claim for damages, of course, but to perform other less unpleasant duties that require professional experience and expertise.

You should seek a solicitor who is capable, expeditious and trustworthy, and whose fees are reasonable. (Some suggestions for selecting a solicitor are outlined in Chapter 10.) There is still no guarantee, however, that at the end of the day, the bill for legal fees will be entirely without surprises. Frequently the bewildering terminology employed by the legal profession extends to the bill for services, which can make interpretation and confirmation of any previously advised fees very difficult.

The bill must give you details of the work your solicitor has done to enable you to see exactly what you are being charged for. A bland statement, 'For Professional Services', is not enough. If necessary, send it back and ask for a more detailed bill.

The amount that your solicitor will be allowed to charge you depends on whether the work she is doing for you involves work in court (called 'contentious' work) or does not involve work in court (called 'non-contentious' work).

In non-contentious work, you can agree beforehand a definite amount that your solicitor is going to charge you, called a 'fixed fee'. If such a fixed fee is not agreed beforehand, then your solicitor is entitled to charge you a fee that is fair and reasonable in all the circumstances. The advantage of a fixed fee is that, however complicated your work turns out to be, you know that you will not have to pay more than the agreed amount. For this reason, it may be difficult to find a solicitor who will agree to a fixed fee if you have anything other than a very routine case. A 'fair and reasonable' fee is more open to argument, however.You can challenge your solicitor's bill for non-contentious work by asking your solicitor to obtain a 'remuneration certificate' from the Law Society.

In contentious work, the situation is complicated by whether you win or lose your case. if you win your case, your opponent will, except in the small claims court, usually be ordered to pay most if not all of your legal costs. Any shortfall not paid by your opponent will have to be met by yourself. If you lose your case, you will have to pay most if not all of your opponent's legal costs as well as your own. In such a case, if your opponent's solicitor is trying to overcharge you, your own solicitor will be able to deal with this. If, however, whether you win or lose, you think your own solicitor is trying to overcharge you, you will be able to challenge her bill. Your solicitor, when charging for contentious work, is, as far as the court is concerned, entitled to the benefit of any doubt about whether it is acceptable to charge you for any particular item. Also, if you expressly or impliedly approved the expenditure on any particular item in her bill, you will not be able to challenge this item, nor any amounts that you approved in advance. However, if your solicitor knew or ought to have known that any unusual item in her bill would probably not be paid by your opponent, she cannot make you pay for this unless she warned you that this might be the case beforehand. You can challenge your solicitor's bill for contentious work by asking the court to approve the bill. This procedure is called 'taxation' of costs. Do not be put off by the name; it has nothing at all to do with the Inland Revenue.

Let us assume then that you have just received your solicitor's bill. It is for more than you expected.

If the discrepancies are minor, and you have otherwise had a smooth journey through the process that precipitated the bill, a telephone call to the solicitor's office will probably be all that is required to clarify the account. But what if the bill defies analysis, what if the amount billed is much more than expected, and you suspect it is not due to an accounting error?

Few clients are eager to cross swords with their solicitors, particularly if they have just demonstrated their skill at subduing the opposition. How you question the account requires careful thought and planning. If the matter your solicitor dealt with was routine and straightforward non-contentious work (but remember that you may not know about any complications, particularly if they were of a purely legal nature), then it would be worth your while to phone other firms of solicitors to find out what they would charge for the same work. If they give you estimates that are considerably lower than the amount your solicitor is charging you, this would suggest that her bill is not fair and reasonable in all the circumstances.

In our example, you do not consider the bill to be fair and reasonable, so you send the invoice back. The logic behind returning an incorrect invoice is quite simple, but none the less important. Sending it back shows tangible evidence of rejection, and puts the onus on the sender to react, as you cannot be expected to pay an account that is no longer in your possession. It is also useful to highlight in colour or underline the items you are querying. A conscientious secretary may not want to send the same bill back if it looks too scruffy. Since it will have to be retyped anyway, perhaps it will be easier to make the corrections at the same time. A small point possibly, but it pays to think of as many angles as possible.

The returned invoice will have to be qualified by an accompanying letter, which might look something like this:

---

34 Skydde Row
Lorscam
FX3 2VP

Ms Angela Deth
Byte, Deth, Kurcing & Mallishus, Solicitors
Gillatine Tower
Virelants Street
Lorscam
FX1 1KT

12 November 1992

Dear Angela

I have received your bill dated 11 November for £1,687.00, covering your acting on my behalf in the matter of drafting the lease for and securing the assets of my recently acquired private zoo.

As far as I was aware, the transaction was no more complicated or prolonged than we anticipated, and I am therefore unable to understand why I have been charged so much more than the

£900.00 you originally estimated. I appreciate that an estimate may be subject to some adjustment either way, but to have almost doubled without notice or explanation is quite unacceptable. I do not consider the amount charged to be fair and reasonable in all the circumstances.

I am returning your invoice herewith. You will note that I have marked the items that I cannot reconcile or that have been charged over the estimated price.

Kindly forward an amended account in line with your estimate of £900.00, and if there are any extraordinary items you feel justified in submitting, please show them separately, and describe them in complete detail in a covering letter.

As soon as I consider the account satisfactory, I will pay it by return of post.

Yours sincerely

Wal Ruses

Encl

If you confirm any estimates in writing prior to engaging the solicitor, any such large increase in the solicitor's fee will be difficult to justify. A detailed breakdown may be a burden to the solicitor, but the greater the detail, the better able you will be to dispute the amounts. Finally, you have promised immediate payment once you agree to the account.

Usually solicitors' fees, although theoretically calculated on a fixed hourly rate, can be negotiated successfully, with the firm still making a handsome profit. For example, a lot of the mundane work in the purchase of your zoo will probably have been performed by a junior, who would command a lower salary. The hourly rate charged to you, however, would not necessarily reflect this. A lot of 'rounding-up' might have also occurred; an eight minute telephone call invoiced at a quarter of an hour, for instance. So there is plenty of flexibility, particularly if you are quite prepared to stand your ground. You might be prepared to show some flexibility yourself; you should probably accept a variance of between 10 and 15 per cent without making too much of a fuss.

Should you not be offered the reduction to which you feel entitled, there are other incentives that can be mentioned in your next letter. Solicitors generally dislike arguing over bills, particularly when the option to involve the Law Society or the courts is offered to them. The fact that you are aware of the existence of both these facilities is well worth mentioning.

But before you send the next letter, you must decide whether to continue to withhold all the amount claimed, or just pay the portion you consider appropriate. If you pay nothing, you will doubtless encourage a quick response, since your solicitor will be keener to collect a larger amount than a smaller one. Also, you will have the benefit of any interest accruing in your account, or the money might be temporarily useful for some other purpose. On the other hand, your solicitor may suspect that you are procrastinating because you cannot afford to pay, or simply do not wish to. You will not want them to doubt your motives and to change their response from defensive to offensive.

If, instead, you remit the amount you are prepared to pay, making it clear that this is absolutely all that she is going to get, you will find your position considerably improved. You will have shown that you do have the money, and are willing to pay, provided a reasonable compromise is possible. If she knows the amount sent is adequate compensation for the work performed, she will probably not wish to engage in further time-consuming correspondence for the balance. Your next letter should therefore be something like this:

---

34 Skydde Row
Lorscam
FX3 2VP

Ms Angela Deth
Byte, Deth, Kurcing & Mallishus, Solicitors
Gillatine Tower
Virelants Street
Lorscam
FX7 1KT

28 November 1992

Dear Angela

I have received your letter dated 26 November, and returned bill dated 11 November. I regret that I cannot reconcile or agree with your justification for the extraordinary difference between your estimate made on 23 September, and the actual amount invoiced.

I therefore enclose a cheque for £900.00 in full and final settlement for the services provided, as per the estimate upon which I based my contract with you, in good faith. Kindly forward a receipt at your earliest convenience, confirming that my obligations to your practice have been met in full.

If I do not hear from you by 5 December agreeing to this, I shall write to you to ask you to obtain a remuneration certification from the Law Society.

I look forward to hearing from you.

Yours sincerely

Wal Ruses

Encl

If the work was contentious work, then instead of saying that you will write to ask her to obtain a remuneration certificate from the Law Society, you should say that you will write to ask her to have her costs taxed by the court.

You have made it very difficult for the solicitor not to agree to your terms since she now has a substantial part of the bill paid, with the threat of the troublesome and time-consuming business of obtaining a remuneration certificate from the Law Society or of taxation by the court if she persists in claiming the balance. The chances of further opposition are therefore very remote.

In non-contentious work, if you ask your solicitor to obtain a remuneration certificate from the Law Society, you must do so within 28 days of receiving the bill. The solicitor will send her file of work on your matter to the Law Society. The Law Society will ask you for your comments on the bill. They will then produce a certificate stating what in their opinion is a fair and reasonable amount to charge. The solicitor must accept this. The procedure is very advantageous to you for the following reasons: the Law Society will not increase the amount of the bill, only decrease it or leave it as it is; the procedure is free; the solicitor cannot charge you extra for her time spent on obtaining the certificate; and the procedure normally takes a few months, during which time you will be earning interest on your money. There is therefore a strong incentive for the solicitor to come to some agreement with you about the bill before this procedure begins.

If the solicitor tries to sue you for an unpaid bill without waiting for you to negotiate, she cannot do so unless she tells you of your right to ask for a remuneration certificate and waits one month before commencing her legal action.

Your letter to the solicitors asking for a remuneration certificate should be to the point. It should be sent within the 28-day period and should be sent by recorded delivery so that you have proof that it was received within the time limit. The letter will look something like this:

---

34 Skydde Row
Lorscam
FX3 2VP

Ms Angela Deth
Byte, Deth, Kurcing & Mallishus, Solicitors
Gillatine Tower
Virelants Street
Lorscam
FX7 1KT

6 December 1992

Dear Angela

I note that you have not been able to agree to my offer set out in my letter to you of 28 November.

Please obtain a remuneration certificate from the Law Society in respect of your bill dated 11 November 1992.

Yours sincerely

Wall Ruses

Once the Law Society has produced a remuneration certificate, if you still disagree with the bill, you can ask a court official to tax the costs, but very few people ever reach this stage. Note also that if you miss the 28-day deadline, you can still ask for the costs to be taxed as if it were for contentious work.

In contentious work, the process of taxation is through a court hearing. Therefore, if you are not confident about attending and speaking at a court hearing, you may not want to carry out your threat, and hope that the threat in itself is sufficient to make your solicitor see sense. The hearing is conducted in private. At the hearing, the court official will have the solicitor's file of her work for you in front of him. He will go through each item in the bill. He will ask for your solicitor's comments and your own comments on whether that item should be allowed. So if you wish to challenge any particular item, you will need to have a good argument to back you up. remember that if there is any doubt about whether any particular item in the bill should be allowed, the benefit of the doubt will be given to the solicitor. The court official will then allow either all or part or none of that item to be charged by the solicitor.

In practice, in the County Court, but not the High Court, a court official will look at the file before the appointment for the taxation hearing is made and decide upon a figure. He will write to you and your solicitor suggesting this figure. If you both agree to this figure, it will save you having to turn up in court for the taxation hearing. You do not have to agree to this figure.

To set the taxation ball rolling, write to your solicitor a letter something like this:

---

34 Skydde Row
Lorscam
FX3 2VP

Ms Angela Deth
Byte, Deth, Kurcing & Malishus,
Solicitors
Gillatine Tower
Virelants Street
Lorscam
FX7 1KT

6 December 1992

Dear Angela

I note that you not been able to agree to my offer set out in my letter to you of 28 November.

Please arrange for an appointment for a taxation hearing and for your bill dated 11 November 1992 and all necessary papers to be lodged in court.

Yours sincerely

Wal Ruses

After the taxation hearing, should you still not be satisfied, you can appeal. Alternatively you can make a complaint to the Solicitors Complaints Bureau. You can only do this once you have complained directly to your solicitor and are dissatisfied with her response. The Bureau deals with a wide range of problems about solicitors and the way they have handled your case, not just overcharging. They produce helpful leaflets and have a useful telephone helpline. See the 'Useful Addresses' section at the back of this book. If you are then dissatisfied with what the Solicitors Complaints Bureau has done for you, you can make a complaint to the Legal Services Ombudsman.

8

Unaccommodating Accommodation: Tenants vs Landlords

Anyone who rents property must deal from time to time with the landlord. Many landlords are quick to respond to their tenants' needs; others need written reminders of their obligations every time a problem arises.

Landlord raises rent unreasonably high

The amount of rent your landlord wants to charge you and the amount you are willing to pay will usually be determined by a number of factors: market forces; whether there is a shortage or surplus of housing in that area; how keen you are to live in that area; how keen you are to live in that particular property; whether the landlord thinks you are a good tenant; whether the landlord is more interested in getting as much money as possible out of the property no matter how many tenants he has than in having one happy tenant who will stay a long time and look after the property; how much security of tenure you have; and so on.

It will often be the case that a landlord will propose an increase in rent and the tenant will, with a grumble, accept it either because the tenant does not realize that he can challenge the rent or because the tenant wishes to remain on good terms with the landlord. But here, as in most walks of life, our lawmakers have decided to intervene and have given some tenants the right in some circumstances to challenge the level of rent.

But before resorting to your legal rights, if any, it is always worth trying to sort things out informally with your landlord. If the landlord regards you as a particularly valuable tenant because, for example, you look after the property well, he will be more agreeable to negotiating with you about the rent. It is always worth a go.

But always bear in mind that if you do not have security of tenure, that is if the landlord can evict you without good reason, you should think carefuly before challenging him about the rent. He may decide he will be better off with a tenant who will not argue about the rent and you will then find yourself without a home.

Never agree either orally or in writing to an increase in rent if you wish to challenge it. If you do agree to it, you may lose your right to challenge it.

If you know of other properties which the landlord owns (for example, the same landlord may own a whole block of flats) ask the tenants of these other properties whether they have had a demand for excessive rent. Even if they have not yet had a demand for an increase, if the landlord demands an excessive amount from you, it is very likely that in due course he will demand an excessive amount from all his other tenants when their turns come. Concerted action by many tenants against the same landlord will put you in a much stronger bargaining position.

The following rough guide to the law is very much simplified, but will cover most private tenants. If your informal negotiations with your landlord fail, you should get advice on your legal rights from a solicitor, a Citizens' Advice Bureau, a law centre or other advice agency before taking action to refer your rent for independent assessment to the Rent Officer, the Rent Tribunal or the Rent Assessment Committee.

In brief, the way that rents in the private sector are controlled by the law is that, in certain circumstances, you can ask an independent body called either a Rent Officer, a Rent Tribunal or a Rent Assessment Committee to look at the level of rent and they will decide whether the level of rent is acceptable or not. To determine which of these bodies and in what circumstances you can have your rent looked at, you will need to take advice from a solicitor, a Citizens' Advice Bureau, a law centre or other advice agency.

The Rent Officer and the Rent Tribunal use similar principles to determine how much you should pay. They will look at the age, condition and location of the property and compare your rent with other rents for similar properties in the same area that they have looked at in the past. They keep a register of these rents and you are allowed to look at this register at any time to see what the rents for similar properties are. If yours is much higher, this is good evidence for asking your landlord to reduce your rent.

The Rent Assessment Committee will compare your rent with the rents for similar leases of similar properties in the same area. They will only reduce your rent if it is significantly higher. They will, however, disregard the effect on the rent of any improvements you have made.

So if you have put in a new bathroom since your last rent increase, you will not have to pay more by virtue only of your new bathroom.

The crucial point to extract from the above is that if you know similar properties in your area are being rented for less, then you have a good argument to use with your landlord. You will be able to tell your landlord this and point out to him that this is the basis on which the rent is independently assessed, and they would therefore decide in your favour should you refer the matter to them.

To find out what similar properties in your area are renting for, visit estate agents, letting agents and accommodation bureaux to enquire, look in your local newspapers and inspect the register of fair rents kept by the Rent Officer (see under 'Rent Officers' in the phone book). This will give you the evidence you need to challenge your landlord.

Say you live in a block of flats. Your flat is one of 12 flats in the block and you share a common landlord. One morning over your bacon and eggs, you read a letter you have just received from your landlord which gives you notice that he is proposing to put up your rent from £350 per month to £420 per month. Even this early in the morning, you can calculate this to be a 20 per cent increase over the year. You cannot remember what the most recent inflation figure was, but it was definitely below 2 per cent. To justify this exorbitant increase, the landlord points out that the car park for the flats was resurfaced last year and that the level of rents generally is increasing greatly. Both of these reasons fail to satisfy you, so after breakfast you sit down and write him a letter something like this:

Flat 4
101 Exorbitant Road
Hardup
HD6 8TP

Mr Gary Abigwolit, MD
Skweazemdry Properties Ltd
90 Menislumms Avenue
Hardup
HD2 8QJ

6 April 1993

Dear Mr Abigwolit

I have received your letter dated 4 April 1993 informing me that you propose to increase my rent by 20 per cent on 1 June 1993.

I note the two reasons you give for the increase, but I regret to say that I find these reasons unconvincing. You will of course be aware that inflation is below 2 per cent, and therefore your proposed increase is more than ten times the rate of inflation.

Perhaps you would be good enough to look again at the proposed increase and reduce it to an acceptable level?

I look forward to hearing from you.

Yours sincerely

Terry Blepour

This is merely a first shot across his bows to show him that you will not meekly pay whatever he demands. This may make him change his mind. It will also allow him to rectify the mistake if it turns out that he has made a mathematical error or wishes to pretend that he has made a mathematical error to save face.

However, in the event, your first letter does not work. The landlord writes back to you repeating that in his view the increase is justified by the improvements and the general level of rents. Now is the time to start using more forceful arguments. Find examples of rents for similar properties in your area. You will then be in a position to dispute your landlord's contention that the general level of rents is increasing. Write to him as follows:

Flat 4
101 Exorbitant Road
Hardup
HD6 8TP

Mr Gary Abigwolit, MD
Skweazemdry Properties Ltd
90 Menislumms Avenue
Hardup
HD2 8QJ

14 April 1993

Dear Mr Abigwolit

I have received your letter dated 8 April 1993 which I found a disappointing response to my letter.

You will be aware that the level of rents of similar properties in this area is good evidence to determine the level of rent payable by me. I have investigated this myself and have found the rents to be in the range from £340 to £390 per month. Your suggested figure of £420 is greatly in excess of even the highest comparable figure. No doubt, if I were to have the rent independently assessed, you would be required to reduce it.

I know my fellow residents in 101 Exorbitant Road will be interested to hear of your new demand for rent, as this will be a problem which will affect all of them sooner or later. If I do not hear from your shortly with a revised offer, I shall make contact with my fellow residents.

Yours sincerely

Terry Blepour

Unfortunately, this fails to impress the landlord and he remains unwilling to reduce his demand. You should first make absolutely sure that you have the legal right, in your particular circumstances, to have the rent assessed by the Rent Officer, the Rent Tribunal or the Rent Assessment Committee by asking a solicitor, a Citizens' Advice Bureau, a law centre or other advice agency. You can also at the same time find out the procedure for doing this.

Now you are in a position to contact your fellow residents. You may already have a tenants' association through which you can raise the matter, but if not you can write to them as follows:

Flat 4
101 Exorbitant Road
Hardup
HD6 8TP

21 April 1993

To all residents of 101 Exorbitant Road

Dear Fellow Residents

As you can see from the enclosed copy letter, our landlord is trying to increase my rent by 20 per cent. I have taken legal advice and I have been advised that I can refer this increase to the Rent Assessment Committee, and it is likely they will order a much lower rent.

I am interested to hear if any of you have received similar demands and are disputing them, or if you are worried that your rent is due to be increased shortly and that you will receive a similarly exorbitant demand.

You will I am sure realize that joint action by as many of us as possible will give us more bargaining power and will also spread the costs of challenging the new rent.

I look forward to hearing from you.

Yours sincerely

Terry Blepour

Encl

Once you have got together with as many of your fellow residents as possible, you can begin the process of legally challenging the increase, now that you have exhausted the informal methods.

Rent rebate for disturbed accommodation

The majority of apartment buildings are designed to comply with building codes and engineering specifications, not necessarily to win design awards. Standards vary according to market influences; buildings will have more facilities and be of better quality in expensive and sophisticated districts than those in areas that are less well off, which will inevitably be reflected in the landlord's rent charges.

Other conditions influence the standard of a particular unit or units, and these include the age of the building, the materials used to construct it, the size of the building, whether it has been converted from an older residential or commercial structure, and its proximity to outside influences that might affect the structure or comfort of the tenants. With an older apartment building, for example, traffic may have steadily increased over a number of years, or an adjoining property might have been adapted for commercial use, raising the noise and pollution levels.

Generally, these are conditions over which the landlord has no control, and it is up to prospective tenants to take such matters into consideration before committing themselves to a lease. Don't complain after moving into the premises about something beyond the landlord's control that was perfectly obvious at the time the unit was inspected. For instance, a basement flat can hardly be expected to afford the same amount of natural light as a flat on the second floor. Such a shortcoming is inevitable, and readily evident before a lease is signed.

Anyone living in a high-density building should be prepared to be tolerant. No building is perfectly designed, is totally soundproofed against noise from outside or fellow residents, or has a magic system whereby necessary repairs are made before the need for them occurs.

Tenants invariably view paying rent with reluctance, and assume that the unfortunate landlord is a millionaire who has never had to do a stroke of work in his life and doesn't care about his tenants. This may be true in some cases, of course, but even if it isn't, the landlord is usually presumed guilty until (and sometimes, even when) proved innocent.

It can be difficult to ensure that all tenants in a building, particularly if it is a large one, will maintain standards at a high level, and you cannot reasonably expect a landlord to be totally successful in his selection of occupants. Inevitably, there are differences in the way various tenants conduct themselves, just as there are differences in the degree of responsibility exercised by landlords.

There are, however, occasions when a complaint is justified, and appropriate steps must be followed in order to obtain a satisfactory outcome without jeopardizing a tenancy agreement or one's relations with the landlord or fellow residents. There is usually a term in your lease requiring you not to be a nuisance, cause noise, and so on, to your fellow tenants. Each of your fellow tenants will probably have a similar term in their lease, and you are entitled to expect your landlord to take action if one of your fellow tenants is breaching this term.

Let's assume that you live in an flat with hardwood floors, fixed to what you presume is a concrete subfloor. You can tolerate the inevitable noises – the odd door slammed in anger, unruly guests visiting a neighbour, someone dropping something. But a new tenant assumed residence in the flat above you three weeks ago, and you haven't slept since. Despite the stipulation in the lease requiring tenants to install sufficient carpeting to prevent noise disturbing other tenants, you are still being disturbed at all hours by footsteps, furniture scraping, things being dropped, and other unidentifiable bangs and clatters.

Three weeks is enough time to allow for unpacking and arranging furniture, and installing a carpet or adequate rugs; you are now entitled to request that your new neighbours afford consideration to their fellow residents. Before confronting your neighbours, however, you should keep a log of the times and severity of the disturbances. This will give your grievance credibility and may prove helpful later.

Your first contact with your neighbours must be carefully worded in order to persuade them that your grievance is very real, that resolving it is important to you, that you are sure that they are probably unaware that noise is so easily carried to adjoining flats, and that you are not the resident 'radar' out to plague every tenant in the building with an endless repertoire of complaints. You could confront them in person, but this is not advisable since a resultant argument will not be to your advantage.

A better route would be to speak to the caretaker first, if there is one, to register your complaint, and then to proceed on your own with a letter. Of course, you will keep the caretaker informed of your progress. Don't contact the landlord or his managing agent yet – give your neighbours the benefit of the doubt.

A short note introducing yourself and describing the circumstances that compelled you to write is your most appropirate course of action. Keep a copy of the letter, of course, but don't send copies to the caretaker or landlord at this stage, as you don't yet know whether their intervention is going to be required. Copies can be included with any subsequent correspondence, if necessary.

Your letter should read something like this:

Flat 609
44 Vaguerant Street
Despair
TH5 3RH

The Occupant(s)
Flat 709
44 Vaguerant Street
Despair
TH5 3RH

23 March 1993

Dear Sir or Madam

As will be evident from my address, my flat is directly below the flat into which you moved at the beginning of March.

I regret that our first contact has to be in the form of a complaint, as I like to think that I am both tolerant and respectful of those with whom I share proximity, but I have to bring to your notice the persistent and disturbing noise that carries through from your flat to my own, presumably as a result of your not having installed carpeting or rugs.

I appreciate that it takes time to unpack and arrange furniture and other household belongings, which is obviously difficult to accomplish in silence, but I do feel that after three weeks, the level of disturbance should be reduced to a minimum.

Please, therefore, install floor covering as necessary, refrain from wearing hard-soled shoes on bare floors, and ensure that movement of furniture and other effects does not transmit excessive noise to my flat, particularly at night.

Thank you in anticipation.

Yours faithfully

Will Ushudddup

There is no need to mail the letter – just slip it under their door or through the letter box if there is one. If your neighbours are responsible citizens, then an immediate reduction in the noise should be apparent. You might even receive a note of explanation or a personal visit to pour oil over troubled waters.

If not, and the disturbance persists, or worse, the noise increases, then you will have to gear up your efforts accordingly. Another, stronger letter is required, and a copy should be handed to the caretaker requesting that he intervene on your behalf to ensure that the tenant complies without delay with the conditions detailed in the letter. Be prepared to back up your complaint with notes from your log. Keep a copy for yourself, of course, but do not send one to the landlord yet. Write as follows:

Flat 609
44 Vaguerant Street
Despair
TH5 3RH

The Occupant(s)
Flat 709
44 Vaguerant Street
Despair
TH5 3RH

27 March 1993

Dear Sir or Madam

My letter of 23 March requesting that you install carpeting and reduce noise in compliance with your lease, so that I might be protected from the excessive and disturbing noise emanating from your flat, has not met with any evident reduction in the noise. On the contrary, the noise appears to have increased, and persists over even longer priods than previously.

Your immediate cooperation in reducing this unnecessary and distressing encroachment is again requested.

Your consideration in complying will be greatly appreciated.

Yours faithfully

Will Ushuddup

cc Ben Dovabakwodz, Caretaker, 44 Vaguerant Street

Ask the caretaker to visit your flat at a time when you know the occupant of the flat above will be at home, to confirm whether the noise is indeed excessive. Insist that you cannot tolerate the noise any longer, and that you will be contacting the landlord if it does not cease. Ascertain the name of the tenants, so that you can address them personally in any further communication.

If there is still no improvement, then a letter to the landlord is required:

Flat 609
44 Vaguerant Street
Despair
TH5 3RH

Mr Justin Itferakwid, MD
Rak Anwruin Properties Ltd
89 Prophit Avenue
Despair
TH5 6WR

29 March 1993

Dear Mr Itferakwid

Since 1 March, when your new tenant, Mr Des Truktiv, assumed occupancy of flat 709, directly above me, my right to peace and quiet has been seriously compromised by continuing loud and disturbing noises emanating from that flat.

The main cause of the noise appears to be Mr Truktiv's failure to install suitable carpeting on the hardwood floor as required by his lease.

I did not register my complaint with Mr Truktiv until 23 March, when I wrote him a short request, since I know moving can be drawn out and I assumed he might need some time to settle his belongings and to purchase a carpet. The noise persisted, however, and if anything became even more pronounced than ever.

I wrote again on 27 March, and at the time gave a copy of my letter to the building caretaker, Mr Dovabakwodz, requesting that he intervene on my behalf. Mr Dovabakwodz also visited my flat and confirmed that the noise from above was indeed excessive.

I have recorded consistent disturbance between the hours of 6.00 am and 8.30 am, and between 6.30 pm and 1.30 am, Monday to Friday, and approximately 16 hours per day on weekends, between 10.00 am and 2.00 am the following morning. This is a total of 79 hours per week, or nearly half of every day! To date there has been no reduction whatsoever in the level of noise.

This is absolutely unacceptable. Please promptly take whatever steps you consider appropriate to restore my right to peace and quiet. Thank you.

Yours sincerely

Will Ushuddup

cc Des Truktiv, tenant
   Ben Dovabakwodz, building caretaker

If the disturbance still persists after three or four days, and you have not been contacted by any of the recipients of your correspondence, ask the caretaker if he has received any instructions from the landlord, and if he has taken any further action on your behalf since you last spoke to him. If he has been asked by the landlord to intervene, and has done so, tell him that while you appreciate his efforts, they have not achieved any results as yet, and request that he speak to the offending tenants again.

If he hasn't heard from his employer, ask him to contact him for advice on how to handle the matter, and to again convey your continuing annoyance to the tenant as soon as possible. If there is still no improvement after a few days, write to the landlord again, as follows:

Mr Justin Itferakwid, MD
Rak Anwruin Properties Ltd
89 Prophit Avenue
Despair
TH5 6WR

10 April 1993

Dear Mr Itferakwid

My letter of 29 March, describing the intolerable noise I have endured in my flat since 1 March 1993, has not produced any response or reduction in the continuing disturbance from the tenants directly above me. Neither have my requests for intervention to caretaker Ben Dovabakwodz proved to be of any benefit.

I am no longer able to endure this serious infringement of my right to peace and quiet in my flat, and cannot understand why nothing has been done to rectify the matter.

Please be aware, therefore, that if the noise has not ceased by Friday, 24 April 1993, I shall be obliged to search for alternative accommodation against my wishes. Until I do move out, I will be invoicing you at monthly intervals for a 45 per cent refund on my rent, which represents the percentage of time my flat is rendered unsuitable for the purpose for which it is intended.

Please also be aware that should I be obliged to move through your failure to ensure that my premises are adequately protected from outside interference, I will be looking to you for all expenses incurred in moving to another address, including loss of wages if time off work is necessary; telephone, electricity, and gas connection charges; transport costs; change of address notifications; and any difference in rent if a comparable new flat is more expensive than my current one.

I trust, therefore, that I may expect some positive action before 24 April, failing which I shall have no option but to initiate the measures stated above.

Yours sincerely

Will Ushuddup

cc Des Truktiv, tenant
Ben Dovabakwodz, building caretaker

The prospect of having to finance your departure, together with receiving bills for rent refunds until you leave, should be sufficient to galvanize the landlord into action. (But don't risk eviction by actually reducing your rent payments.)

Instant silence should not be expected – it takes a few days to arrange carpeting. However, it would be reasonable for Mr Truktiv to reduce the noise until the carpet does arrive. If by 24 April, however, you have still not received a positive response from Mr Itferakwid, then you must serve notice of your intention to move, and send your first invoice. In fairness to the landlord, you should invoice for your inconvenience only from the date you first notified him of the noise.

Mr Justin Itferakwid, MD
Rak Anwruin Properties Ltd
89 Prophit Avenue
Despair TH5 6WR

24 April 1993

Dear Mr Itferakwid

Further to my letter of 10 April, I am disappointed to inform you that to date you have failed to address my very real concerns, and that the excessive and intolerable disturbance from the flat directly above my own continues unabated.

In consequence, therefore, and against my will, I am obliged to seek alternative accommodation that offers me the peaceful occupation to which I am legally entitled. As soon as I have secured a suitable flat, I will serve formal notice of my intended date of vacation.

Meanwhile, I enclose my invoice for the suffering and inconvenience experienced to date, and incurred through your having failed to manage the building to standards required from a responsible landlord. Early settlement wil be appreciated.

Yours sincerely

Will Ushuddup

Encl
cc Des Truktiv, tenant
Ben Dovabakwodz, building caretaker

It is important that you continue to send copies of your letters to all parties who are in a position to contribute a solution to the dispute. Notification of your increasing despair may yet produce the action needed to stay your intended departure. And should subsequent court proceeedings be required, no one will be able to claim that they understood the matter to have been resolved.

It is not necessary to send duplicates of the invoice with the copy letters; notification that you are makiing a claim is quite sufficient. The invoice may look something like this:

Will Ushuddup
Flat 609
44 Vaguerant Street
Despair
TH5 3RH

Rak Anwruin Properties Ltd
89 Prophit Avenue
Despair
TH5 6WR

24 April 1993

For the attention of Justin Itferakwid, MD

INVOICE

For: Rental rebate for Flat 609, from 29 March to 22 April 1993, for failing to allow peace and quiet through landlord failing to take action against unacceptably noisy tenant in Flat 709, who moved in on 1 March 1993.

Noise level persists for at least 45% of the time. Thus:

Monthly rent	£875.00
45% of rent =	£393.75
Amount due	£393.75

Terms: Net monthly. Overdue accounts attract interest at 1.5% per month.

Such an ominous letter and invoice should convince the landlord that something must be done, and you will be able to settle the matter before actually having to give notice and move out.

If your demands are not complied with, and you decide to move, continue to send invoices every month until you do leave. If you really prefer to stay, and the landlord refuses to refund the 45 per cent include a statement with your second invoice, detailing the overdue £393.75, plus 1.5 per cent interest of £5.90, plus current invoice of £393.75, and type prominently, 'Unless this account is settled in full by Friday, 5 June 1993, a court summons will be issued without further notice', at the bottom of the page. If he still fails to respond, issue the summons.

Should you decide to move, you should serve written notice of vacation as soon as you find new premises, giving the landlord as much time as possible to find a new tenant. If the notice is less than the legal minimum requirement, then the reason must be included in your notice, as follows:

Flat 609
44 Vaguerant Street
Despair
TH5 3RH

Mr Justin Itferakwid, MD
Rak Anwruin Properties Ltd
89 Prophit Avenue
Despair
TH5 6WR

3 June 1993

Dear Mr Itferakwid

I shall be vacating the above flat on 30 June 1993, against my will because of the disturbing and unacceptable noise levels that have deprived me of my legal entitlement to peace and quiet since 1 March 1993.

I remind you that numerous written and verbal complaints to you, your caretaker, and the tenant responsible for the noise have not met with any success in resolving the problem.

In the circumstances, I cannot be held responsible for the amount of notice given, since my move is dictated by conditions outside my control. My moving expenses will be forwarded to your office for settlement.

Yours sincerely

Will Ushuddup

cc Des Truktiv, tenant
Ben Dovabakwodz, building caretaker

As soon as you are settled in your new flat, send the invoice for all your moving expenses to the landlord. Remember to keep all the applicable receipts, as they may be needed later to verify the amount claimed. The invoice for the move should look something like this:

Will Ushuddup
32 Haven Street
Despair
TH4 3SP

Rak Anwruin Properties Ltd
89 Prophit Avenue
Despair
TH5 6WR

6 July 1993

For the attention of Justin Itferakwid, MD

INVOICE

Re: Flat 609, 44 Vaguerant Street, Despair

For: Moving expenses, from above premises on 30 June 1993

Removal charge	£287.50
Connection fees, telephone, electricity, gas	£83.34
Notifications of address change	£38.00
Lost wages during moving	£65.00
Difference between old and new rent (old rent £875.00 per month, new rent £918.00 per month) (1 year lease=12×43.00)	£516.00
Total:	£989.84

Terms: Net monthly. Overdue accounts attract interest at 1.5% per month.

If none of the previously sent invoices have been paid, to save yourself the trouble of sending a final statement at a later date, you could give notice with this invoice that a summons will be issued for the total outstanding amount, unless full settlement is received by the end of the month.

There will always be a landlord somewhere who fails in his obligations and refuses to compensate tenants or correct any deficiencies that are his responsibility, no matter how hard the injured party pleads. In which case, a carefully recorded and correctly administered campaign to obtain satisfaction should receive a favourable judgement in the courts.

Your holiday is ruined

The glossy brochures that advertise holidays tend to exaggerate the resorts they are trying to pitch. Pictures of golden beaches – deserted except for the perfectly tanned and scarcely attired model – blue skies, luxurious rooms, tables piled with delicacies, vintage wines, and exotic cocktails, as well as quaint local scenes, are intended to lure travellers. However, reality does not always match these descriptions; you may find littered beaches packed with people, hotels barely completed, adverse weather, and inedible food.

The exaggerated hyperbole of holiday brochures ('the holiday of a lifetime') cannot be used to substantiate a claim in law. None the less, there must be no factual inaccuracies in the brochure description, and a reasonable level of service must be given. The accommodation must be as close to the beach and amenities as advertised, the food should be palatable, and the hotel efficiently maintained and operated, and pleasant to stay in. If a particular service is intolerably substandard, what can you do to obtain an improvement? Complain, obviously. But how and when? And if the remedy is inadequate, how do you obtain compensation?

Assume you are holidaying overseas for two weeks. The trip is a package tour, booked in your home town. When you arrive at your hotel, you notice immediately that your room is extremely dirty. The bath has rings around it, the cups are dirty, giant dust balls cover the floor under the bed, and the atmosphere is scarcely neutral! Since hotel rooms are typically cleaned most thoroughly in the time between when guests depart and new ones arrive, you are concerned the condition will only get worse.

So before you even unpack, you seek out the manager and ask him to accompany you back to your room, where you voice your indignation over the lack of cleanliness in such a way that translation will not be required even if language is a barrier. It is important to do this right away, since he will be more likely to respond to a new guest that to one who has already put up with things as they are for some days.

Do not unpack until the room has been cleaned to your satisfaction. If nothing is done within an acceptable period, find the manager again, and interrupt him no matter how busy he is elsewhere. If you are sufficiently indignant and persistent, he should quickly be persuaded that it is futile to ignore you. If he still dawdles, take your bags to the reception desk and continue your argument in public, where the commotion is sure to attract an audience. The manager will not be enthusiastic about having to defend his laxity in full view of other guests, diners, visitors and staff, and he will probably act immediately to placate you. You might even take with you to the lobby a dirty cup, bag of dust balls, or filthy towel to create more impact. You will probably end up with the cleanest room in the hotel! If there is a tour representative for your package tour, you should also complain to her, and ask her to press the manager to find you another room.

If this still does not produce the cleanliness you require, or if it is not maintained during the rest of your stay, you may want to seek damages from the tour operator when you get home. In order to justify any claim to which you may feel entitled, it is vital you voice your complaints to the manager and the tour representive continually during your stay, at least once a day, in the hope that something may be done and that you have a record to show the tour operator that you did everything you could to obtain an improvement. Take photographs. Keep notes of the times you complained and to whom you spoke, what was promised, and what actual inconvenience you suffered. Determining how much to seek in compensation will be difficult, and will depend on how dirty the room actually was and to what degree it affected the enjoyment of your vacation.

Since you probably spent no more than two or three waking hours a day in the room during the holiday, you would probably not be entitled to a refund of a big percentage of the total cost of the trip. None the less, the lack of cleanliness preyed on your mind, even when you were away from the hotel, and affected your enjoyment. You should seek a reasonable amount, one that does not make you appear greedy, yet high enough to prevent future problems for other tourists – 10 to 15 per cent of the cost of the trip might be in order. Once you have determined an amount, you will send a letter to the tour operator.

---

85 Spotless Lane
Nogermsin, Mysink
HG6 6YA

Mr Perry Grinate, MD
Mann Ovabord Tours Ltd
22 Flezenlice Street
Leftin, Ahury
TY5 2SA

1 December 1992

Dear Mr Grinate

My wife and I have just returned from a two-week stay in the Hotel Sordide on the Costa Ransome, booked through your company as the enclosed copy invoice will confirm.

I regret to inform you that our stay was ruined by the appalling lack of hygiene practised by the hotel which, despite our combined daily efforts itemized on the enclosed list, continued to plague us until the day we left. This is the first time I have had occasion to complain to your otherwise excellent company, and I have no doubt an organization with your reputation will want to launch an immediate investigation into the operation of this hotel so that future clients will not have to endure a similar unpleasant experience.

I am sure you will want to offer compensation for our grossly inadequate accommodation, as per the enclosed list of complaints and invoice for what I hope you will agree is a reasonable rebate under the circumstances.

Please let me have your observations with the remittance, as well as your assurances that our experience will not be repeated on future holidays with your organization.

Thank you in anticipation.

Yours sincerely

Drew A Blanc

Encl

The letter confirms that you are a regular client, and that you will continue to patronize the tour operator if you are compensated at the requested level. Enclose your invoice thus:

Mr & Mrs Drew A Blanc
85 Spotless Lane
Nogermsin, Mysink
HG6 6YA

Mann Ovabord Tours Ltd
22 Fleezenlice Street
Leftin Ahury
TY5 2SA

1 December 1992

For the attention of Perry Grinate, MD

INVOICE

Re: Holiday for two persons, 14 days/nights at Hotel Sordide, Costa Ransome, your reference HS/56456

Total amount paid	£3,456.00
Compensation required for suffering due to grossly inadequate hygienic conditions at hotel, detailed on separate enclosed list.	£345.60

Terms: net monthly. Overdue accounts attract interest at 1.5% per month.

Also enclose the list of your complaints and your attempts to have them rectified, and what results your efforts produced, something like this:

Your Reference HS/56456, Hotel Sordide, Costa Ransome

List of Complaints

17 November. Arrived at hotel. Complained three times to manager, Mr Idi Otte, and twice to your tour representative, Ms Hope Less, about filthy toilet, cockroaches, litter, dirty sheets, no light bulb in bedroom. Nothing was done.

18 November. Complained four times to manager, three times to receptionist and three times to your tour representative. Room still has filthy toilet, cockroaches, litter, dirty sheets, no light bulb in bedroom. Still nothing was done. (And so on.)

By the time you have covered 14 days' worth of inconvenience, the list will look most impressive, and should evoke ready sympathy and a refund from the tour operator.

Most tour companies will listen to their customers and will want to satisfy reasonable complaints. If you are dealing with a company of doubtful repute, and they are not willing to see your point of view, then a more strongly worded letter may be required.

---

85 Spotless Lane
Nogermsin, Mysink
HG6 6YA

Mr Perry Grinate, MD
Mann Ovabord Tours Ltd
22 Flezenlice Street
Leftin, Ahury
TY5 2SA

7 December 1992

Dear Mr Grinate

I am in receipt of your letter dated 6 December and I am sorry to read that you do not appear to consider your company responsible for the inadequacy of hotels provided for your clients. I am quite unable to accept the contents of your letter, and hold you fully liable for the suffering my wife and experienced through your failure to monitor the facilities offered by Hotel Sordide.

Kindly, therefore, be aware that unless my invoice for £345.60 is settled in full by Wednesday, 18 December 1992, a summons will be issued wihout further notice.

Yours sincerely

Drew A Blanc

cc Ellie Fant, MD, Association of British Travel Agents
Hugo Farr, MD, Fluds, Fammin & Pestilants Travel Agents Ltd

Send copies of the complete correspondence to the travel agent through which you booked the holiday. Find out if the tour operator is a member of the Association of British Travel Agents (ABTA). If it is, it will certainly say so on the holiday brochure. If it does not appear from the brochure to be a member of ABTA, phone the travel agent, the tour operator or ABTA and ask them whether the tour operator is a member of ABTA to confirm your facts. If it is a member of ABTA, then you should also send copies of the correspondence to ABTA, by way of a threat to the tour operator. This should encourage Mann Ovabord to settle your bill.

If the bill is not settled, you have a choice. You could either issue a summons in the small claims court or, if the tour operator is an ABTA member, you could take advantage of ABTA's arbitration scheme. The ABTA scheme is a documents-only arbitration. You must present your arguments on paper as there is no hearing. In the small claims court, however, you will be able to present your case in person before the judge. If you do not feel you can adequately get your arguments across in writing, the small claims court would be the preferred option.

Both methods will cost you some money, and it is worth finding out from ABTA and the local County Court what the current charges are, as this will be an influencing factor on your choice.

Unlike the above example, if the problems you experienced were so bad that they effectively ruined your holiday, then you can ask for *more* than the cost of the holiday by way of compensation for the suffering you and your family have experienced.

9

Fear of Flying: Taking on the Airlines

Although advertisements consistently proclaim that airlines provide trouble-free travel to their passengers, problems can and do arise.

Overbooked flight

Airlines routinely overbook flights to compensate for 'no-shows' – the passengers who book a flight and don't show up. If the predicted number of overbooked passengers don't appear, the airline is relieved that it can indeed accommodate all the passengers who do. Occasionally, however, the system backfires – the no-shows show up – and the airline must 'bump' passengers off the flight. The normal bumping procedure is for the airline in question to ask for volunteers who are willing to stand down in exchange for compensation, which varies from one company to another. If too few volunteer, then the airline may select passengers to stay behind against their wishes. Passengers flying during peak travel periods may be especially at risk.

If you are unlucky enough to be bumped against your wishes, you need not accept whatever compensation the airline offers you, even if the airline tries to convince you that the compensation they offer is standard for the circumstances, and is not negotiable. Fellow passengers may accept the airline's offer, but you do not have to comply just because they have. Whatever the purpose of your trip, be it holiday or business, you are entitled to claim damages. But since you have yet to depart for your destination, you are not in a position to know the amount of inconvenience the delay is going to cause, so negotiating compensation is extremely premature, rather like negotiating a divorce settlement during a wedding ceremony!

Imagine that you and your spouse are looking forward to a long-overdue and well-deserved two-week holiday in Tenapenny. You have survived the frenzied last-minute packing, the mad dash to the airport, and the seemingly endless wait at the check-in counter, and you are both now in the departure lounge eagerly awaiting your departure to a warmer climate. By noon local time tomorrow, Thursday, you should be lounging on the beach.

Suddenly, an announcement informs the expectant gathering that, due to unfortunate circumstances, there are insufficient seats to accommodate the number of passengers booked on this particular flight. The message offers profuse apologies, and requests that eight passengers volunteer to wait for the next flight. A few minutes later, there is a request for more volunteers, since only four travellers have decided to accept a delay in their schedule. Soon after, the crackled voice names four people who are to report to the boarding representative. Your names are among the four.

With mounting apprehension, you approach the desk, where the representative informs you, again with profuse apologies, that since you were among the last passengers to book this flight, you will have to step down and take the next available flight. Your protests are greeted with sympathy, but the decision is final, and you are given no choice but to resign yourselves to your fate.

You are guaranteed a reservation on the next flight, which is at 3.30 pm tomorrow, which means you won't arrive in Tenapenny until early Friday. The airline offers to accommodate you at their expense in a nearby hotel, including £50.00 each for meals and incidentals, and free transport to the hotel and back. If this suits your immediate requirements, go ahead and accept the airline's offer, but make quite sure the representative understands that your acceptance is not to be interpreted as full settlement and that you will be submitting a claim when you return from Tenapenny in two weeks.

Do not sign any standard documentation that may impede your right to seek further damages. If the airline insists that you sign a waiver in order to qualify for the compensation, you should refuse to do so. You will instead organize your own overnight lodging, and add it to the final bill upon your return. In this case, however, the company has bowed to your insistence, filed the waiver unsigned, and you go to your temporary lodging.

The next day all goes smoothly: you make it to the airport on time, the flight leaves on schedule, and you finally arrive at your Tenapenny hotel in time for a continental breakfast on the patio of your hotel. After two weeks away from it all, you arrive home, and it is time to consider your claim against the airline.

You still had to pay the hotel in Tenapenny for the missed first night, which, since it was booked separately from your flight, is easy to calculate. And you lost holiday time, which is not as easy to put a monetary value on. But you decide to claim for the cost of a day's

accommodation and meals. Once you have determined the amount of your claim, send a statement of your account as follows:

---

747 Beach Avenue
Iskapism
HG4 2MT

Mr Bud Jerigar, MD
Fryteflite Airlines Ltd
Hijaque Building
Zepallin
FG4 8KT

20 April 1993

Dear Mr Jerigar

On Wednesday, 1 April 1993, at approximately 2.30 pm, my wife and I deposited our luggage with your check-in desk at Chambels Airport, and made our way to the departure lounge, where we confidently waited to board your flight number FF 786, scheduled to leave for Tenapenny at 4.30 pm. To our astonishment and dismay, 30 minutes before our intended flight, we were told by your airport representative, a Miss Emma Jency, that our reservation would not be honoured because your company had accepted bookings in excess of the number of seats available. Despite our protests at this unexpected and appalling treatment, we were forced to take a flight the next day.

Our eagerly awaited holiday was both shortened and disrupted. We had to spend an unwanted night in an airport hotel. When we finally arrived at our destination, we found that your disgraceful performance had ruined the pleasure of our holiday.

I hold your organization entirely responsible for the losses we have incurred through your negligence, and enclose our invoice for immediate settlement.

Yours sincerely

Phil Ourpursiz

Encl

The invoice accompanying the letter should look something like this:

Phil and Lyne Ourpursiz
747 Beach Avenue
Iskapism
HG4 2MT

Fryteflite Airlines Ltd
Hijaque Building
Zepallin
FG4 8KT

20 April 1993

INVOICE

For expenses and inconvenience suffered through denial of boarding flight number FF 786 on 1 April 1993.

Loss of 1 day hotel accommodation and meals in Tenapenny. (Total cost of 14 days/nights £1,820.00)	£130.00
Loss of enjoyment and disruption of holiday	£250.00
TOTAL	£380.00

Terms: Cheque by return of post. Overdue accounts attract interest at 1.5% per month.

Most airlines will settle expenses that have been inflicted through their deliberate policy of overbooking aircraft seats. After all, this policy resulted in a full payload on your original flight, and the amount you are claiming in compensation is less than the price of your two return fares.

However, if the airline dithers, a further prod might expedite matters. Write something along these lines:

Mr Al Battros, Chairman
Fryteflite Airlines Ltd
Hijaque Building
Zepallin
FG4 8KT

27 April 1993

Dear Mr Battros

My letter and account of 20 April, addressed personally for the attention of your MD, Mr Bud Jerigar, has yet to be accorded the courtesy of a reply.

I am sure you will agree that the matter demands immediate attention, and I therefore trust you will take urgent steps to ensure that the matter is resolved without further delay.

I look forward to your early settlement, and thank you in anticipation.

Yours sincerely

Phil Ourpursiz

cc Bud Jerigar, MD

The copy to the MD will warn him that the chairman is about to enquire why his valuable time has been imposed upon for a trifling claim of £380.00! As usual, you have given few details so that the chairman will be forced to find out what is going on. Your persistence should result in a quick settlement, but if not, another letter is in order.

---

747 Beach Avenue
Iskapism
HG4 2MT

Mr Bud Jerigar, MD
Fryteflyte Airlines Ltd
Hijaque Building
Zepallin
FG4 3KT

4 May 1993

Dear Mr Jerigar

I have received your letter dated 1 May 1993, confirming that your company is concerned only with making as much profit as possible, with no interest or consideration for your unfortunate passengers.

Unless my account for £380.00 is settled in full by Tuesday, 19 May 1993, a court summons will be issued without further notice.

Yours sincerely

Phil Ourpursiz

cc Al Battros, Chairman

It is unlikely that the airline will want to risk unnecessary bad publicity, particularly since their chances of winning in court are slim. Fortunately, most reputable airlines will capitulate well before threats of legal action become necessary.

You arrive - but your suitcase doesn't

When you check your baggage in at the airport, invariably you wonder, if only subconsciously, whether you will ever see it again. Happily, the majority of suitcases do get on the same flight as their owners, or if they go astray, the airlines usually find them within a day or so, and return them safely to their anxious owners.

Some precautions will help ensure that your luggage arrives when you do:

- Avoid using expensive luggage, especially if travelling in poor countries – thieves may be eager to discover whether the contents are equally opulent. Use a shabby suitcase instead.
- Do not put faith in suitcase locks. Most can be easily opened.
- Once your suitcases have been searched, tie them up with lots of string. A thief is not going to start untying string on a shabby suitcase when there is an undefended expensive suitcase nearby for him to pilfer.
- Make sure your luggage is sound, because it may be subject to vigorous treatment on its journey, and a defective suitcase may not last the trip.
- Remove all old labels and tags to avoid confusing baggage handlers. Check-in attendants usually do this as a matter of routine, but you should make sure the job has been done before your cases disappear down the conveyor belt.
- Look carefully at the tags the check-in attendant puts on your cases. They usually have the name of destination printed on them. Is it correct?
- Don't check in at the last minute – your bag may not make it on board, even if you do. In which case, you can only hope that the airline will be good enough to send it on the next flight. If the baggage is subsequently lost, any claim that you might have for compensation may be less than watertight.

If you take all these precautions, your luggage may arrive when you do! If, despite these precautions, your luggage is lost, then the airline will have to provide compensation.

Most airlines have a fixed compensation schedule for such loss, which varies from company to company, and which may not cover your losses. Such guidelines do not have to be taken at face value, however, and passengers should be entitled to the cost of replacing their property and any other losses that were suffered as a consequence. Most holiday insurance policies will cover lost luggage and the purchase of essential items if luggage is delayed. But check your policy carefully about notifying the police and get proof of the notification.

Say your suitcase fails to arrive on the carousel after your flight. All the other passengers have collected their bags and departed. You find a representative of the airline and report the loss immediately. They will have a standard procedure for tracing anything that has been misplaced, and there is not much else that you can do other than leave the matter in their hands. After you have supplied all the details required, take the name and telephone number of the representative, who will in turn have recorded the address and telephone number of your destination.

You should ask whether the luggage will be sent to you as soon as it is located, or whether you will be expected to collect it. If you are told that you will have to return to the airport to collect it, make it clear that your travel expenses in doing so will be the responsibility of the airline, in which case they may decide they would prefer to deliver it instead!

Point out that you will need certain items that were in your suitcase immediately, and the longer you are without it, the more replacements you will be obliged to purchase or hire. Leave no doubt that all your expenses will have to be covered by the airline, which will give them the option of supplying you with some of the items you require, or suggesting where they may prefer you to make any purchases or to hire anything.

Whether your luggage has been temporarily misplaced or permanently lost, try to do what is most reasonable and appropriate for both parties, without inconveniencing yourself unduly. Say you are on a skiing trip, for instance, and you naturally expect to venture on to the slopes first thing tomorrow morning. It would hardly be interpreted as fair and reasonable if you purchased brand-new equipment, when quite adequate substitutes can be hired just as easily. Your own luggage might arrive safely at the end of the first day's stay, so hiring rather than buying should be the preferred option for most items, unless you know for certain that your cases have been lost or stolen.

The airline will do its best to locate your missing luggage, and your cooperation is necessary to reinforce your subsequent claim with sound evidence of goodwill. Before you hire or purchase an expensive item, for instance, phone the representative to check whether the airline has succeeded in finding your baggage, and to see if they have any suggestions as to the most expedient way of obtaining your latest requirement.

Maintaining a log of all your attempts to keep your (their) expenses to a minimum will greatly enhance the chances of your settling your claim without serious contest. Keep all receipts, including those for transportation to and from hire shops or retailers where you had to obtain replacements. When you have completed your holiday or business trip, type up a list of your expenses, and send it in the form of an invoice, with a covering letter to the airline, as follows:

---

23 Frateloss Avenue
Pillferring
RT3 3UB

Mr Bau Ingg, MD
Pan Demonium Airlines Ltd
1 Kramptseetz Place
Jettlagd
HC5 9LB

4 December 1992

Dear Mr Ingg

The enjoyment of my annual ski trip last month to Kraktribbs Mountain Resort received a severe setback when my baggage was inadvertently sent to San Taklaus by Pan Demonium Airlines instead of accompanying me on flight PD328 to Ruttd Tarmaak Airport, on 17 November.

I had to wait four days, until the evening of 21 November, for my suitcases to be retrieved and returned to me, which as you may imagine, was extremely irksome and inconvenient, particularly since I was carrying new and expensive skiing equipment.

During this time, although I managed as best I could without several personal effects, I was obliged to hire and buy some essentials to tide me over, as discussed on each occasion with your very helpful representative at Ruttd Tarmaak, Ms Helen Hiwater. This is the first time I have ever been parted from my luggage in many years of flying, and I am surprised that it happened on one of your flights, for I have always found your service to be very efficient and competitive.

I enclose my bill for the expenses incurred as a result of this unfortunate incident, and, as I am sure you will agree, I have succeeded in keeping unavoidable expenditure to an absolute minimum, considering the circumstances. Your early settlement will be greatly appreciated.

Yours sincerely

Lisa Pearovskeez

Encl

The invoice should look like this:

Lisa Pearovskeez
23 Frateloss Avenue
Pillferring
RT3 3UB

Pan Demonium Airlines Ltd
1 Kramptseetz Place
Jettlagd
HC5 9LB

4 December 1992

INVOICE

For expenses and inconvenience suffered through the loss of suitcases for four days from flight number PD328 on 17 November 1992

	£
Replacement items:	
Toiletries	16.00
Clothing	74.50
Ski Pass	88.00
Hired items for four days' hire:	
Skis	65.00
Protective ski clothing	55.00
Ski boots	38.00
Camera	28.00
Incidental expenses of arranging replacement and hire	33.00
Inconvenience and loss of enjoyment	150.00
Total	£547.50

Terms: payment within seven days. Overdue accounts attract interest at 1.5% per month.

Enclose copies of the receipts and keep the originals. The airline is entirely at fault for losing your luggage; your letter has shown that you are a regular flier who prefers to travel with Pan Demonium, and your invoice shows that you kept costs to a minimum. This combination should ensure that early reimbursement will be made.

In the unlikely event your claim is disputed, drop a line to the chairman as follows:

---

23 Frateloss Avenue
Pillferring
RT3 3UB

Mr Roy Alairforss, Chairman
Pan Demonium Airlines Ltd
1 Kramptseetz Place
Jettlagd
HC5 9LB

8 December 1992

Dear Mr Alairforss

I am in receipt of a letter from your MD, Mr Bau Ingg, which informs me that Pan Demonium Airlines does not accept responsibility for expenses incurred by passengers when their possessions are lost through mishandling by your baggage handlers.

I would be greatly obliged if you could confirm that Mr Ingg has misinterpreted company policy toward those unfortunate enough to suffer losses for which your airline is entirely liable.

Perhaps you would also be kind enough to inform Mr Ingg that unless my invoice dated 4 December for £549.50, is paid in full by Monday, 23 December 1992, a summons will be issued without further notice.

Yours sincerely

Lisa Pearovskeez

cc Bau Ingg, MD

It is doubtful that the airline will want to risk going to court and losing a case in which they have no defence and that may attract adverse publicity. A cheque should therefore soon be on its way.

If Pan Demonium persists in denying your claim, then issue the summons as promised. This will convince them that you are serious, and mean to be paid. They will probably settle before a court appearance becomes necessary.

10

If All Else Fails

The principal purpose of this book is to show you how to settle claims through written communication. Occasionally, however, you may have no alternative but to take your case to court.

The small claims court

The procedure for making a small claim in the small claims court is relatively straightforward and is outlined below. If you are claiming a substantial amount of money, and particularly if it looks as though your case will go to trial, you should seek more specific and detailed advice from a solicitor (but don't forget you will not be able to recover her costs in the small claims court even if you win), a Citizens' Advice Bureau, a law centre or other advice agency.

In cases where you are claiming a fixed sum of money from another person, as in the examples in this book, you would start your action in the High Court or the County Court or the small claims court. The small claims court is often talked about as though it were an entirely separate court, but in fact it is a part of the County Court.

For your purposes, you can forget the High Court. You would need to be claiming more than £50,000 or have an exceptionally complex case before you could use the High Court.

Claims for amounts below £1,000 will be dealt with by the small claims court. For amounts over £1,000 you would normally use the County Court, but if you and your opponent both agree, you can use the small claims court instead.

There are many advantages to using the small claims court: it is cheap; it is informal; it is held in private; and, except in very unusual circumstances, you will not be ordered to pay your opponent's legal costs. Throughout the case, you, who are making the claim, are known as the plaintiff, and your opponent is known as the defendant.

Look in the telephone directory under 'Courts' for the address of your nearest County Court. The County Court is open from Monday to Friday, 10 am to 4 pm. Go along to the court office and tell them you want to start an action in the small claims court. They will give you three copies of the summons, Form N1. The fee payable for issuing the summons will depend on how much you are claiming, so tell the court clerk the amount you are claiming and ask how much the fee will be. The fee varies from a minimum of £10 up to a maximum of £70 (1993 fees).

You will need to fill in the summons Form N1 three times (one copy for yourself, one for the defendant and one for the court). Take the forms away with you so you can fill them in at your leisure which will give you time to think about what you are going to say on the form. The form asks you for details of your claim. If you need help filling in the trickier parts of the form, ask at the court office, or take it to a Citizens' Advice Bureau, a law centre or other advice agency.

When it is filled in, take the forms back to the court. Hand them in at the court office and pay the fee. The court will stamp them, give one back to you, keep one for itself and the court will send the third one to the defendant. The defendant has 14 days, counting from the day after he receives the summons, to do something about it. In due course, the court will tell you on Form N205A when the defendant has received the summons.

If the defendant completely ignores the summons, you can ask the court to 'enter judgment by default'. To do this, you need to fill in the bottom of Form N205A, 'Request for Judgment'. Part C of the form will ask you how you want the defendant to pay: immediately, by such and such a date or by instalments. Think about whether the defendant can afford to pay it all at once; it may be better to get it paid by instalments. Send the bottom portion of this form to the court.

The court will then send a Form N30, 'Judgment for Plaintiff' to the defendant and a copy to you. This is a court order ordering the defendant to pay. If he ignores this order, you will be able to take action to enforce this order (for example, by using bailiffs).

If the defendant replies to the summons, he will either (1) admit the full amount of the claim and either send a cheque to the court or ask for time to pay; or (2) he can admit part of the amount claimed and dispute the remainder; or (3) he can deny all of the claim. He may also make a claim against you. These are dealt with in turn.

If the defendant admits the full amount of the claim, but asks for time to pay, he will fill in Form N9A in which he will say he will pay the amount on a specified future date or he will propose paying by instalments. You must decide whether to accept his offer or demand more immediate payment, and tick the relevant box on your Form N205A, 'Request for Judgment'. If you want him to pay more quickly, you put down the payment schedule that would be acceptable to you, and send it to the court together with his Form N9A. The court will look at his proposed payment schedule and your proposed payment schedule and decide which to accept or make a compromise. The court will fill in its decision on either Form N30(1) or N30(2) and send copies of this form to you and to the defendant. He must follow the court order. He must pay on time. If he doesn't, you can take action to enforce the judgment (for example, by using bailiffs). You can appeal against the court's decision on the payment schedule.

If the defendant admits the claim, he may send a cheque for the full amount to the court. This is relatively rare. When the cheque clears, the court will pay the money over to you.

If the defendant admits part of the claim but denies the rest, he will fill in Form N9A in respect of the admitted part and the 'Defence' on Form N9B or on the back of Form N9, with his reasons for disputing the rest. The court will send a copy of the form to you. You can accept the part that he has admitted and argue about the payment schedule. If you do not accept his defence, the matter will have to go to trial, and the case will be transferred to the defendant's local County Court.

If the defendant disputes all of your claim, he will say so by filling in the 'Defence' on Form N9B or on the back of Form N9. The court will send a copy of the form to you, the case will be transferred to the defendant's local County Court and the case will go forward to trial.

It is possible in the last two cases for the defendant to make a claim against you, called a counterclaim. He will do this on Form N9B, but in the cases we are discussing in this book, this is unlikely to happen.

If your case is going forward to trial, the next step will be either the issue of automatic directions or a preliminary hearing. Automatic directions are used in most cases. They are instructions from the court on how the case is to proceed from here. They are specified in detail on Form N450, which the court will send to you. They lay down a timetable for matters such as compiling and exchanging a list of all relevant documents in your possession (such as invoices, letters etc) and exchanging copies of witness statements. You will in due course need to apply to the court for a date for the trial to be fixed.

In exceptional cases, instead of the court issuing automatic directions, there will be a preliminary hearing. You will be notified of this by the court. The hearing is informal and is held in private. You must attend this hearing or your case will probably be dismissed. But you can take a friend along with you. If the defendant does not turn up, you can ask for judgment against him at the hearing. If you both turn up, the judge will attempt to settle the case there and then. If he cannot, he will give instructions on how the case will proceed from there and will set out a timetable. A date for the trial will be fixed at the hearing.

At the trial, matters will proceed in private and informally, usually with the parties sitting around a table with the judge. There will probably be no lawyers present, so there will be little chance of your being intimidated by a hotshot, high-powered lawyer. Most judges are helpful and are sympathetic to people conducting their own cases. If there is anything you do not understand, ask the judge for an explanation. You can take a friend or an advice agency worker with you, who can speak on your behalf, but you must also be there. You cannot send someone along in your place.

The judge will make his decision and if it is in your favour, the defendant will be ordered to pay you in due course. A payment schedule will be worked out. If he does not pay on time, you can take steps to enforce your judgment (for example, by using bailiffs).

There is no right of appeal against the judgment, except in very unusual circumstances.

Finding a good solicitor

Finding a good solicitor who has sound experience in your particular type of claim can be a surprisingly difficult task. If you do not know a solicitor or have never used one before, you risk selecting one for all the wrong reasons.

You can of course find solicitors listed in the Yellow Pages. But how do you choose the right one for you? Solicitors' names and phone numbers say nothing about their competence. And ads luring clients with vague promises are no help either. A 'free initial consultation' may be a genuine and generous offer by a highly competent solicitor who is setting up a new practice, or it may indicate a bad solicitor who has to offer incentives to drum up business. 'Fees you can live with' may in fact send you into instant bankruptcy, but you would presumably still be alive to enjoy the experience! The Yellow Pages, then, are not the best place to look for a solicitor.

If you know someone who works in the legal profession, she might be able to put you in touch with someone suitable. But she will likely recommend the solicitors who work for her firm out of loyalty to her employers, which is not much better than using the Yellow Pages.

Would it be worth contacting a 'celebrity' solicitor, one whose name is regularly in the news or who writes books or columns? Probably not. Their fees, which will have risen to reflect their elevated status in the community, will likely be prohibitive, and some lawyer-authors may not have time for serious practice any more.

Your best option is to get recommendations from friends or colleagues whose judgment you can rely on. Or you can contact a

Citizens' Advice Bureau, or a law centre or other advice agency, if there is one in your community. They will be able to give you the names and addresses of solicitors in your area who claim to practice in the area of law in which you are interested. They will not, however, be able to *recommend* any particular solicitor.

Solicitors have different strengths and specializations; a property solicitor, for example, may not have the knowledge to successfully bring a claim for personal injury in a car accident. So try to ascertain the strengths of the solicitors recommended to you, and whether they have successfully handled cases like yours. You could find someone who had what appeared to be an iron-clad case, which was entrusted to an experienced and proven solicitor, but was beaten, despite all efforts, by the defendant's lawyers. You then ascertain the name of the victor, and offer him or her your case!

When you find someone who appears competent and experienced in your type of claim, make an appointment to discuss the case in detail and how the solicitor charges for his work. Make a list of all the questions you need answered before the meeting, leaving space for the answers, so there are no doubts or grey areas after you leave the office. Feel free to ask anything you think important; you will not want any unexpected surprises when the case is well under way. There is no reason that reputable solicitors shouldn't welcome a potential client's interest in their way of working, and if they are evasive or vague, then you should probably take your business elsewhere.

You should enquire about your chances of success, how long the proceedings are expected to take, whether there is a chance to settle out of court, and so on. Will the solicitor accept phone calls at home, or only during office hours? Does she spend a lot of time in court, honing her skills? Will she handle the case herself, or will part of it be looked after by a junior colleague? Will she adhere rigidly to your wishes, and seek permission to deviate? Will she keep you up to date on all developments?

If you are satisfied on all fronts, then you can verbally inform the solicitor you will be pleased to have him or her act on your behalf, and confirm all the details in writing, including your understanding of the terms and conditions you discussed. Write something along these lines:

---

36 Planetiv Avenue
Casty Gate
FG3 9RS

Willie Suem
Wrritt, Harras, Flogg & Suem, Solicitors
Court Towers
Brybeville
WL4 8NS

4 March 1993

Dear Mr Suem

Further to our pleasant meeting this morning, I enclose all details of my claim against the International Kolerah Hotel, which you have kindly agreed to conduct on my behalf.

I have noted for my records your fees of £43.00 per hour, which will be billed to me on a monthly basis, and that you anticipate complete recovery of my costs from the defendants, in the event of our winning the trial. I understand that you will keep me informed of events as they transpire, and consult with me as often as necessary. Should a compromise be desirable, in your opinion, I understand you will fully acquaint me with the details and reasons *prior* to any agreement with defendants or their solicitors.

Please let me know if I can offer you any further information. I look forward to your regular reports that this case is proceeding to an early and successful conclusion.

Best regards.

Yours sincerely

Wilf Uldamige

Encls

Your letter confirms exactly what your expectations are, and reminds him that you are not abandoning the case to his discretion and that you intend to keep fully abreast of his progress.

Make sure things get under way as soon as possible, and check with your solicitor as necessary to ensure that the momentum does not slacken off. Don't become a nuisance, with daily phone calls at inconvenient times. A few regular phone calls at appropriate stages will do.

When discussing any strategy or point that requires your decision, make sure you fully understand the solicitor's explanation of the subject. If the terminology is obscure legalese, get him to translate the information into layman's terms.

You should also do your part – keep your solicitor informed of any developments he may not be aware of, let him know if you expect to be away for more than a few days, let him handle the case as discussed, and pay your bills as agreed. Providing you maintain a good working relationship, you should be able to pursue your claim to a satisfactory conclusion.

Legal costs

In a court case like those mentioned in this book, a solicitor will work out how much to charge you by keeping a record of how much time she spends working on your case and multiplying this by an hourly rate. This means that the more time-consuming your case is, the more you will have to pay. It also means that if you phone your solicitor every day and keep her talking for half an hour on the phone, you will find yourself landed with a very large bill!

Your solicitor will add on to her bill her disbursements, that is her out-of-pocket expenses such as court fees. She will also add on VAT to her own costs and to some of the disbursements.

Your solicitor will, unless you are a regular client of hers, usually want her money in advance (called 'costs on account'). When all this money is used up, she will want more before she continues to work on your case. When you pay your solicitor money in advance, she will pay it into a special bank account. When she sends you a bill, she will then transfer the same amount of money from this special bank account into her own bank account in satisfaction of her bill.

You should ask your solicitor to send you a bill every month or every three months. This will enable you to keep a track of how much money is being spent, because if you do not, the bills will mount up and you may find yourself owing a small fortune to your solicitor. If necessary, place a limit on the amount of costs your solicitor can run up, and tell her that she needs to seek your express permission to exceed that amount.

If you pursue your claim in the small claims court, you will not usually have to pay your opponent's legal costs if you lose, only your own, though you may have to pay your opponent's other expenses. If you pursue your claim in the County Court and you lose, you will usually have to pay most if not all of your opponent's legal costs as well as your own. Of course, conversely, if you win in the small claims court, you will not be able to claim your legal costs from your opponent, though you may get some of your other expenses paid, whereas if you win in the County Court, your opponent will usually be ordered to pay most if not all of your legal costs. These are factors to bear in mind when you decide which court to sue in or indeed whether to sue at all.

If you think your solicitor is overcharging you, you can challenge this in the ways set out in Chapter 7.

When you go to see a solicitor for the first time, there are various schemes on offer which may save you money if you can take advantage of them.

Your solicitor may advertise a free initial consultation which will usually last about half an hour which you can use to discuss your case to see if she thinks you have a case worth pursuing. Your solicitor will not normally do any work for you, such as writing a letter, in this half hour. She will merely sit in her seat and chat with you about your case.

If your claim is for personal injury you could go to a solicitor who is a member of the Accident Legal Advice Scheme. The Law Society, your local Citizens' Advice Bureau, law centre or other advice agency will be able to give you the name and address of a solicitor in your area who is a member of the scheme. The scheme will allow you half an hour's free consultation with a solicitor during which you can discuss your case with her and she will be able to advise you on whether you have a case that is worth pursuing.

Another alternative is to ask for a 'fixed-fee interview'. This is an interview with a solicitor which lasts a definite length of time, usually half an hour, for which you pay a fixed reasonably small amount, usually between £5 and £30, in advance. You know that, provided you do not go over your allotted time, you will not have to pay more than the agreed amount. You can use the interview to discuss the case with your solicitor. The majority of solicitors will no longer do fixed-fee interviews, but some will and the Law Society, your local Citizens' Advice Bureau, law centre or other advice agency should be able to tell you which do. The amount charged and the length of the interview will vary from one firm of solicitors to another, but at the time of writing it is still possible to find solicitors who will give you half an hour for £5. Make it clear to your solicitor when you make the appointment that you want to see her under the fixed-fee interview. Otherwise you may be charged a full commercial rate.

If you are running a business and the claim that you are making is being made as part of your business, you will be able to take advantage of the 'Lawyers for Business' scheme. The Law Society will be able to give you the names of solicitors in your area that are members of the scheme. The scheme will give you half an hour's free consultation with a solicitor to discuss your case.

In all the instances mentioned above, you are limited by time, in most cases to half an hour. This precious time will slip by very quickly, so it is vital to prepare yourself in advance to make the best use of this time. Write down all the relevant facts beforehand so that you have them ready at your fingertips. Write down all the questions you want to ask so that you don't forget anything. Gather together all the documentation, however remotely connected, and sort it out into date order, the earliest first, and take it with you to the interview. In the interview, stick to the point! Do not give your solicitor a complete history of your life for the past five years; most of it will be irrelevant.

If your claim is for personal injury, you may consider taking advantage of the new 'conditional fee' scheme. As this scheme is new it is not clear how popular it will be among solicitors, as it represents something of a gamble both for you and the solicitor alike. The scheme works as follows. If you lose your case, you will not have to pay any of your solicitor's own costs because your solicitor has agreed to forgo these costs. You will, however, still have to pay any disbursements (such as court fees) and expert witness fees, and you will of course still have to pay your opponent's costs. If, on the other hand, you win your case, you will have to pay your solicitor twice her normal fee, or three times, or one and a half times, or whatever you have agreed between you beforehand. As your opponent will be ordered only to pay most of your solicitor's usual costs (that is, once over only), this means that you will end up having to pay the rest. This could swallow up all your winnings and still leave you with more to pay. Discuss the implications of this scheme with your solicitor before agreeing to it.

Getting help with legal costs

If you are on a low income and have little savings, you may be able to get help with your legal costs. There are two schemes run by solicitors to help you with this: the Legal Aid scheme and the Green Form scheme. If you do not yet want to start court proceedings, but simply want your solicitor to write letters and negotiate on your behalf or help you conduct your own legal case yourself, you should use the Green Form scheme.

To find a solicitor who is willing to do Legal Aid and Green Form scheme work, you can ask the Law Society, your local Citizens' Advice Bureau, law centre or other advice agency for the name and address of a solicitor in your area who does Legal Aid work. Alternatively, adverts in the local press and the Yellow Pages may help you to find one. Fewer and fewer solicitors are willing to do Legal Aid work, because it does not pay very well, but there are still some around who will.

Legal Aid will pay some or all of the costs of bringing your claim. You need to apply for Legal Aid by filling in an application form, and it is usually a good idea to get your solicitor to fill in this form for you. You will have to pay your solicitor to do this but you may be able to get this done as part of a fixed fee interview (see above) or under the Green Form scheme (see below) or your solicitor may do it for free, knowing that she will get a lot of work out of it later on.

To qualify for Legal Aid, you need to be both financially eligible (you will have to take a means test) and have a reasonably good case (your solicitor's help here will be very useful in persuading the Legal Aid Board, who administer the system, that your case is worth pursuing). You will not be allowed to bring unreasonable claims (for example, you could not use Legal Aid to sue someone for a £10 debt, no matter how good your case would be).

Even if you are granted Legal Aid, it may not cover all your costs, and you will then have to pay the rest yourself (called your 'contribution').

If you win your case, except in the small claims court, your opponent will be ordered to pay most, though possibly not all, of your legal costs. The remainder of your costs will be paid by any contribution that you have made. If there is still a shortfall, the Legal Aid Board will take this out of any compensation that you have won. So if your claim is for a relatively small amount and your legal costs are relatively high, even though you won your case you may find yourself with nothing to show for it at the end of the day, and you will quite rightly consider the whole case to have been a waste of time, apart from the satisfaction of a moral victory. Your solicitor will explain how this will affect your particular case, but it is one more factor that will influence your decision whether to bring the case or not.

Alternatively, if you do not intend to start court proceedings, you can use the Green Form scheme. When you go to see the solicitor tell her at the start of the interview that you want help under the Green Form scheme. She will fill in a form (coloured green!) asking for details of your income for the past week and your savings, so make sure you have these details with you. She will be able to tell you there and then if you qualify for any help. There is a limit of two hours on the amount of time your solicitor can spend on your case under the scheme, but your solicitor can apply to have this limit extended.

Under the Green Form scheme, if, as a result of your solicitor's efforts, she successfully recovers money for you, she will deduct her costs that the Green Form scheme covered out of this money and hand over the balance to you. This means that if your claim is for a relatively small amount it may not be worth using the Green Form scheme. Ask you solicitor to explain how this will affect your particular case.

11

The Author is Put to the Test!

In November 1991, I was finally persuaded to succumb to the attractions of electronic technology, and so, suitably anaesthetized for the ordeal, I ventured in the direction of a computer shop, where the entire contents of my wallet was painlessly exchanged for the latest in high-tech wizardry! The reason I made this rash and untypical expenditure was to give my ancient manual typewriter a well-deserved retirement, and to make the writing of this book a more comfortable and efficient experience.

This was the first computer I had ever used, let alone owned, and I consequently treated it with every possible consideration, to ensure any malfunction would not be the result of mistreatment on my part. The components were carefully unpacked and assembled in a temperate and stable area, earthed immediately, and no drink or foodstuff was ever allowed near the work area. In fact, I used it infrequently until the beginning of 1993.

I was, therefore, surprised and concerned when, in February 1993, the monitor began to malfunction occasionally; the screen would black out for a few seconds or minutes, recover, and then continue to operate normally. Since I had no idea whether this was an indication that something was amiss, or whether computers were prone to the occasional cough or stutter, I called the shop that had sold it to me for an opinion. The service manager was most helpful and knowledgeable, and informed me immediately that the power supply was probably failing, and that I could expect the problem to worsen and the computer to expire sooner or later.

I expressed surprise at this premature failure, and explained that the unit had experienced very little use since its purchase. It is reasonable to expect a good quality computer to last more than 15 months. I asked whether I could therefore expect it to be repaired at the expense of the manufacturer.

The inevitable answer was that the one-year warranty had expired, and that I would have to pay for the repair myself. The manager was sympathetic, but explained that he was obliged to adhere to the warranty conditions imposed by the manufacturer. I informed him that, although I appreciated his position, I was not impressed by the performance of my machine, and that I did not consider it to have been of merchantable quality because it should last longer than 15 months and that I would be writing to his head office to discover whether they would be prepared to consider my grievance. The manager wished me luck, but warned me that in his long and varied experience my chances of obtaining satisfaction were very slim indeed. I then sent the following letter to the head office.

---

2 West Street
Middlemarch
Loamshire
MW4 3EG

Mr Mike Wrochipp, MD
Lemon Computer Stores Ltd
53 Servis Road
Terminal Corners
HJ4 8ST

2 April 1993

Dear Mr Wrochipp

I purchased a Cardigan GT from the Lemon Computer shop, in Middlemarch on 17 November 1991.

Although, as matters transpired, I didn't seriously start to use the computer until the beginning of February this year, I did use it to type the occasional letter in the interim, and there is no doubt that I am enormously impressed with its capabilities.

However, on 26 February this year, the monitor started to black out occasionally, and I called the service manager of the Middlemarch shop, who diagnosed the problem to be a failing power supply. The screen still blacks out for a few minutes every few days, but thus far I have not taken any steps to repair it. I am told that the repair would not be covered by warranty, since the unit is more than a year old. However, since by my calculation it has been used for only 150 to 200 hours from new, and it has not been moved or mistreated in any way, and was only 15 months old when the fault developed, this must be a fault that occurs more readily than one might suppose. This suggests to me that the computer was not of merchantable quality.

Under normal commercial use, my 200 hours would be reached after only five weeks, which would have been covered by normal warranty.

I should very much appreciate hearing that you are able to authorize the Middlemarch shop to carry out the necessary repair at no cost to myself, under the circumstances. The serial number is S34987658765378, and if you wish to send a representative to confirm the condition and slight usage of the unit, please let me know.

Thank you in anticipation.

Yours sincerely

Bruce West

The letter was duly dispatched, and while I waited for a response, I called a friend of mine, a computer engineer who used to work for the company that manufactured my machine. He confirmed that it did sound as if the power supply was at fault. However, since he had not worked for that manufacturer for some time, he did not know whether this particular model was prone to unreliability.

But, as a starving author engaged in the very act of describing the most expedient procedures for combating unfair trading practices, I knew that if I failed to pursue this one to a satisfactory resolution, I would never be able to look myself in the monitor again!

Then, on 5 April, before I had received any acknowledgment or reply to my letter, the monitor suddenly blacked out permanently, and I was obliged to take it back to the computer shop. They were able to confirm that the power supply needed replacing, and I left the unit for repair. Unfortunately, after it was repaired, collected and paid for, it didn't work at all, and I had to go back yet again to have a loose cable tightened! As soon as this additional service had been performed, all was happily back to normal.

A reply to my letter finally arrived on 16 April, from the 'acting MD', who, as accurately predicted by my two advisers, informed me that 'we will have to decline your request for a free repair'.

Among the numerous reasons for refusing liability was this intriguing sentence: 'Computers can be affected by many outside causes such as electrostatic discharge (static electricity received from walking across a carpet), electrical storms, radio frequency interference, power surges or dips, and other inconspicuous events.'

I carefully resisted the temptation to point out that, to the best of my knowledge, my computer had not yet fully mastered the art of 'walking across a carpet', and replied as follows:

---

2 West Street
Middlemarch
Loamshire
MW4 3EG

Mr Mike Wrochipp, MD
Lemon Computer Stores Ltd
53 Servis Road
Terminal Corners
HJ4 8ST

19 April 1993

Dear Mr Wrochipp

Further to my letter of 2 April, regarding my Cardigan GT serial no S34987658765378, the power supply failed completely on 5 April, and was replaced at your Middlemarch shop. When I arrived home with the repaired unit, it would not work at all, and I had to take it back again the following Monday, 12 April, when the very helpful engineer diagnosed a cable that was not properly connected. He informed me that the cable had 'crept' under expansion and contraction, and had thus disconnected itself, and that this was not an uncommon problem.

I am, incidentally, in receipt of a letter from your Mr Hans Uporichute, the second paragraph of which suggests several circumstances as possible reasons for the premature failure of my machine. My machine has not been subjected to any of the stated events, and even if it had, the power supply is the most robust part of a system unit and would not have been affected. Any properly designed power supply should last indefinitely, which suggests that the Cardigan GT suffers from a design fault. Clearly it was not of merchantable quality.

Perhaps Mr Uporichute would be good enough to confirm that none of the mishaps he listed could have been inflicted on my unit during its long journey from the manufacturers in Singapore to England, prior to my purchasing it. I see no validity in your argument, and enclose my invoice for the expenses and inconvenience that I have suffered through your faulty product.

Yours sincerely

Bruce West

Encs

The invoice accompanying the letter included a photocopy of the work order and paid invoice from the computer shop.

---

2 West Street
Middlemarch
Loamshire
MW4 3EG

Mr Mike Wrochipp, MD
Lemon Computer Stores Ltd
53 Servis Road
Terminal Corners
HJ4 8ST

19 April 1993

For the attention of Mr Wrochipp, MD

INVOICE NO 2121/91

For repair to Cardigan GT No S34987658765378, premature failure of power supply	£185.50
Transport to and from repair shop, correspondence, etc.	£53.70
Loss of time (two and a half days) during repair, nominal amount	£50.00
Total	£289.20

Terms: Cheque by return of post. Overdue accounts attract interest at 1.5% per month.

The letter and invoice were sent the same day, and I anticipated an interesting response to my latest riposte!

This came, unexpectedly, and in the form of a telephone call, from a young lady at the head office whose name and status I didn't ascertain. She informed me that the company had received my letter and invoice, and that they were prepared to pay for the power supply, but not the additonal £103.70 for my incurred expenses. I asked her to put any proposals in writing, and I told her I would respond accordingly.

'You don't want us to send you the cheque now?' she asked. She sounded incredulous that the offer of money was not being gratefully accepted.

I repeated my request for any offer to be sent in writing, and that I would then consider its merits. She agreed to my request, and our conversation concluded without further discussion.

There were several reasons I didn't discuss the offer, or accept it, over the telephone. First, I wanted the details of our dispute on paper, to eliminate any possibility of accidental 'memory loss'. Second, a quick decision during a brief telephone conversation might be regretted later; considering the written offer at leisure would give me more opportunity to assess its merits. Third, I had corresponded with the MD, and a telephone call from an employee whose authority I could not evaluate was not a satisfactory response. Had she offered to settle for the full amount, I would no doubt have gratefully accepted. Finally, my insisting that they go to the trouble of writing to me again increases the possibility that they will tire of the relentless correspondence, capitulate, and send me a cheque for the full claim.

If they do send me the full amount, I will of course be pleased to accept it. On the other hand, if the offer is just as described on the telephone and does not include my expenses, I am also prepared to settle for that. I will have had the computer repaired free of charge, which was my main objective and, although I daresay with persistence I might be able to obtain complete settlement, I think their offer is reasonable, and I am prepared to respond in the same vein.

So no matter how many experts advise you that you won't be successful, no matter how daunting the prospects of failure, persistence can and does produce results.

12

Useful Addresses

Banks

The Banking Ombudsman
Citadel House
5–11 Fetter Lane
London
EC4A 1BR

Building Societies

The Building Societies Ombudsman
35–37 Grosvenor Gardens
London
SW1X 7AW

Cars

Customer Relations Adviser
Society of Motor Manufacturers and Traders
Forbes House
Halkin Street
London
SW1X 7DS
For cars still under the manufacturer's warranty.

The National Conciliation Service
Retail Motor Industry Federation
9 North Street
Rugby
CV21 2AB
For complaints about used cars, repairs and services.

Customer Complaints Service
Scottish Motor Trade Association
3 Palmerston Place
Edinburgh
EH12 5AF
For complaints about used cars, repairs and services in Scotland.

The Conciliation Service
The Vehicle Builders and Repairers Association
Belmont House
Gildersome
Leeds
LS27 7TW
For complaints about car body repairs.

Citizens' Advice Bureaux

See under 'Citizens' Advice Bureaux' in the phone book.

Courts

See under 'Courts' in the phone book.

Electricity

The Office of Electricity Regulation
Head Office
Hagley House
83–85 Hagley Road
Birmingham
B16 8QG
See the back of your electricity bill for your local OFFER office and your local Electricity Consumers' Committee.

Gas

The Office of Gas Supply
Southside
105 Victoria Street
London
SW1E 6QT
Contact first the local office of the Gas Consumers' Council. See the back of your gas bill for the address.

Insurance

Association of British Insurers
51 Gresham Street
London
EC2V 7HQ
For complaints about insurance companies.

The Insurance Ombudsman Bureau
City Gate One
135 Park Street
London
SE1 9EA
For complaints about insurance companies.

Personal Insurance Arbitration Service
Chartered Institute of Arbitrators
24 Angel Gate
London
EC1V 2RS
For complaints about insurance companies.

The Insurance Brokers Registration Council
15 St Helen's Place
London
EC3A 6DS
For complaints about insurance brokers.

Lawyers

The Law Society
113 Chancery Lane
London
WC2A 1PL
For information about solicitors. 071–242 1222

Solicitors Complaints Bureau
Portland House
Stag Place
London
SW1E 5BL
For complaints about solicitors.
Helpline 071–834 8663/4

General Council of the Bar
11 South Square
Gray's Inn
London
WC1R 5EL
For information and complaints about barristers.

Council for Licensed Conveyancers
Suite 3
Cairngorm House
203 Marsh Wall
London
E14 9YT
For information and complaints about licensed conveyancers.

Legal Services Ombudsman
22 Oxford Court
Oxford Street
Manchester
M2 3WQ
For complaints about solicitors, barristers and licensed conveyancers.

Legal Aid

Legal Aid Board
6th Floor
29–37 Red Lion Street
London
WC1R 4PP

Office of Fair Trading

Office of Fair Trading
15–25 Bream's Buildings
London
EC4A 1PR
The OFT produces lots of leaflets and information about a wide range of consumer problems.

Rent

See under 'Rent' in the phone book for the Rent Officer, the Rent Tribunal and the Rent Assessment Committee.

Travel

Association of British Travel Agents
55–57 Newman Street
London
W1P 4AH
For complaints about travel agents and tour operators.

Trading Standards Department

Look for 'Trading Standards' under the entry for your local authority in the phone book.

Telephone

Office of Telecommunications
Export House
50 Ludgate Hill
London
EC4M 7JJ
You must use BT's own complaints procedures before contacting Oftel. Phone BT on 150 to make your first complaint.

Water

Office of Water Services
City Centre Tower
7 Hill Street
Birmingham
B5 4UA

You must use the water company's own complaints procedure before contacting Ofwat.